THE WALL STREET
TRAFFIC LIGHT

A POWERFUL AND SIMPLE INVESTMENT STRATEGY FOR 401(K)S AND IRAS

John K. Harris

Published by The Wall Street Traffic Light, LLC.
(6667 S. Jamestown Place, Tulsa OK 74136)

ISBN 978-0-9801914-8-6

Library of Congress Control Number: 2007910136

Printed in the United States of America by Fidlar Doubleday.

10 9 8 7 6 5 4 3 2 1

For information regarding special discounts for bulk purchases, contact:
The Wall Street Traffic Light, LLC, at thewallstreettrafficlight@cox.net.

To my friend Louise Brown who, in November 1996, provided the impetus for this book by asking, "Is now a good time to sell my stock funds?"

CONTENTS

◇◇◇◇◇◇◇◇◇◇◇◇

PART ONE

Understanding the Wall Street Traffic Light Model

PART TWO

Using the Wall Street Traffic Light Strategy

PART THREE

Developing and Testing the Wall Street Traffic Light Model

◇◇◇◇◇◇◇◇◇◇◇◇◇◇◇◇

INTRODUCTION

◇◇◇◇◇◇◇◇◇◇◇◇◇◇◇

The U.S. stock market is a wonderful thing. Anyone can own shares in American companies and participate in the growth of the largest economy in the world. Some people have less than a thousand dollars invested in U.S. stocks, while others have literally billions of dollars at work there. Fortunes have been made (and lost) in the stock market, and that will continue to be true.

While investing is open to everyone, successful investing is a rather exclusive club. Experienced investors have learned, and novice investors quickly discover, that the results of investment decisions do not always meet expectations. Whether experienced or not, all investors face the same three fundamental questions:

1. *When* to invest in U.S. stocks?

2. *When not* to invest in U.S. stocks?

3. *How* to invest in U.S. stocks?

The Wall Street Traffic Light, a new investment strategy explained in this book, provides specific answers to those questions. The strategy is best suited to 401(k) and IRA investors (because of their tax advantage), but other investors may find it to be useful too.

The Wall Street Traffic Light (WSTL) strategy is based on historical patterns of the S&P 500 Index—the broad-based, large-company index of U.S. stocks that serves as a widely-used barometer of the market. By looking closely at the annual returns and short-term movements of the S&P 500 over time, I found recurring patterns that will help guide investors today. In this book you will discover this important, scientifically-tested history lesson: Over the long term, the WSTL strategy has achieved *higher returns with lower risk* than merely buying-and-holding the S&P 500. That is "sleep well" performance indeed.

You might ask, who am I to set forth such an investment strategy? Well, think of the WSTL strategy as the result of a "numbers guy" turning an analytical eye on the S&P 500. Before my retirement, I was professor of accounting at the University of Tulsa; I hold a Ph.D. in accounting and was a CPA for 25 years. Since retiring I have become somewhat of a stock market historian. In recent years, my research has appeared in *Barron's* (published by Dow Jones & Company). I independently engage in stock market research and receive no compensation to promote any investment product.

As you will discover, this book contains ample numerical support for the basic workings of the WSTL. I expect that some readers will parse every chapter and review all of the calculations. For others, understanding the fundamentals of when to invest in U.S. stocks (that is, when the WSTL is "green") and when not to invest in U.S. stocks (when the WSTL is "red") will be enough. I wrote this book for both types of readers. As a result, the WSTL strategy should be of interest to anyone involved in the U.S. stock market—individual investors, financial advisers, market strategists, professional money managers, academicians and financial journalists.

This book is organized into three parts. Part One (Chapters 1-4) introduces the WSTL model and reviews its powerful performance for 1970-2006. Part Two (Chapters 5-7) guides investors in using the WSTL strategy as a tool to help manage their 401(k)s and IRAs. Part Three (Chapters 8-11) develops and tests the WSTL model, and then discusses the significance of the test results.

To highlight the most important contents, this book features "power points" at the beginning of each chapter. And a companion website is designed to assist investors as they use the WSTL.

John K. Harris

ACKNOWLEDGMENTS

◇◇◇◇◇◇◇◇◇◇◇◇◇◇

Seven talented friends with varied backgrounds added much value to this book. Kip Karney (a microbiologist), Charles Long (an engineer) and James Aldag (a financial adviser) made numerous comments that improved the book's organization and content. Paul Mueller (an attorney) did detailed editing of several drafts and gave helpful feedback on content. Sandy Leeds, senior lecturer in finance at the University of Texas at Austin, provided important comments that added clarity and technical accuracy. Professor Srikant Datar of the Harvard Business School encouraged me to pursue the type of research that led to the development of the WSTL model and helped me obtain historical data. Professor Jim Payne of the University of Tulsa developed the companion website, thewallstreettrafficlight.com.

Others provided helpful feedback on various drafts of the manuscript as well as research assistance. I thank Scott Armbrust, David Bocanegra, Del Chesser, John Ford, Tommy Goodwin, Dean Graber, Lisa Hanold, Gordon Nielsen, Robert Prechter, Dick Roberts, Dorothy Smirle, Bruce Stivers and William Wallace. Mike Moran offered me on-going encouragement.

I thank my wife Judith for her patience and assistance throughout the years of research and writing.

I thank God for blessing me with the ability and opportunity to do this work.

PART ONE

UNDERSTANDING THE
WALL STREET TRAFFIC LIGHT MODEL

Chapter 1

◇◇◇◇◇◇◇◇◇◇◇◇◇◇◇

A POWERFUL AND SIMPLE
INVESTMENT STRATEGY

The following "power points," listed in the order in which they appear in the chapter, alert you to the most important contents. Power points are provided in every chapter.

Power Points

1. The core concept of the WSTL model is reversion to the mean, which works like a powerful magnet pulling the S&P 500's annual returns down after periods of above-average returns and pulling its annual returns up after periods of below-average returns.

2. The WSTL model is based on the S&P 500's annual returns and its short-term movements during 1935-1969. Then, the model's predictive ability was tested for 1970-2006.

3. For 1970-2006, the WSTL strategy achieved higher returns with lower risk compared to buying-and-holding the S&P 500. That powerful performance was accomplished with only 13 trades out of and back into the S&P 500.

4. The main driver of the WSTL model's successful trades for 1970-2006 was the decline of the S&P 500 while the WSTL was red.

5. The WSTL strategy's "alpha" was greater than 2.82 percentage points.

6. My estimate is that less than 10 hours a year is needed to use the WSTL strategy.

The WSTL strategy gets its name from an imaginary Wall Street Traffic Light that alternates between *green* and *red*. When the WSTL turns green, it is a signal to 401(k) and IRA investors to "go" buy the S&P 500. The **S&P 500** is the broad-based, large-company index that comprises approximately 75% of the total value of the U.S. stock market.[1] When the WSTL turns red, it is a signal to "stop" investing in—to sell—the S&P 500 and move those proceeds into 3-month Treasury bills or a money market fund.

The watchword of the WSTL model is "sell and buy lower." Specifically, that means the 401(k)/IRA investor makes a round-trip trade by selling a low-cost S&P 500 index fund and buying it back later at a lower price. The WSTL model made a round-trip trade (on average) once every three years during the years 1970-2006. In most cases, there are *no transaction costs* on either end of the trade, if the S&P 500 index fund used is a mutual fund rather than an exchange-traded fund. In all cases, there are *no tax consequences* in your 401(k)/IRA for any year in which a trade occurs.

In a simple, scientific test, the WSTL strategy achieved powerful performance for 1970-2006: higher returns with lower risk than buying-and-holding the S&P 500. To put the WSTL's performance in perspective, keep this statistic in mind: For any 20-year period, only a small number of mutual funds have achieved higher returns than the S&P 500, and rarely have any of those market-beating funds also had lower risk than the S&P 500. Although past performance is no guarantee of future results, the WSTL strategy has the potential to *accelerate the growth* of your 401(k)/IRA and *reduce the downward fluctuations* in its value—a "sleep well" combination indeed.

Buy-and-hold investors have a "green light" 100% of the time to keep a chosen percentage of their portfolios in the S&P 500. In comparison, the WSTL was green approximately 80% of the time during 1970-2006. Therefore, the 20% of the time when the WSTL was red accounted for the difference in the performance of the two strategies.

As you read the first few chapters of this book, keep in mind that you can choose the "level of involvement" with the WSTL model that best suits your needs. At one extreme, you can regularly visit thewallstreettrafficlight.com to monitor the color of the WSTL. The brief commentaries available there will let you know precisely when the color is expected to change and actually does change. The green and red signals simplify the challenge of investing in the U.S. stock market. You can carry out the WSTL strategy on your own or with the assistance of a financial adviser. At the other extreme, you can learn all of the details about the model in this book. In particular, a high level of involvement should appeal to experienced individual investors, market strategists and financial advisers.

Reversion to the Mean

There is a strong force in the stock market (and all financial markets) called **reversion to the mean**. Under this force, periods of high returns have a tendency to occur after periods of lower returns, and periods of high returns tend to be followed by periods of lower returns. The result is that returns over, say, any 20-year period tend to have an *arithmetic average* (a *mean*) which is nearly the same as their long-term mean. The S&P 500's mean annual return for 1935-2006 was 13.0%.

Consider this distribution of the annual returns for that period:

S&P 500 Annual Return	Number of Years during 1935-2006
Equal to or better than 17.0%	34
9.0% to 16.9%	9
Equal to or worse than 8.9%	29
Total	72

The shaded area is an eight percentage-point band around the mean of 13.0%. Only 9 of the 72 years (12.5%) had a return in that band. Thirty-four years were above the band and 29 years were below it—an almost symmetrical distribution.

What the distribution does not indicate is that clusters of years having above-average returns were preceded and followed by one or more years of below-average returns. In other words, the S&P 500's mean of 13.0% worked as a powerful magnet that sometimes pulled returns down and other times pulled them up.

A recent example, the 1994-2003 period, demonstrates reversion to the mean. The S&P 500's return for 1994 was 1.3%; the returns for 1995-1999 ranged between 21.0% and 37.4%; the returns for 2000-2002 ranged between −9.1% and −22.1%; and 2003's return was 28.7%. While the S&P 500's returns over those 10 years were extremely volatile, they averaged 13.0%—exactly the long-term mean.

Since the S&P 500's annual returns revert to the mean, wouldn't you love to know *in advance* the specific years in which reversion will occur and will not occur? *The WSTL model's forecasts concerning reversion to the mean were accurate for 29 of the 37 of the years during 1970-2006.* Even for the eight years when the forecasts were inaccurate, the WSTL investor suffered financially compared to the buy-and-hold investor in only two years.

Today's conventional wisdom says that the stock market is unpredictable on a short-term basis. For example, Burton Malkiel, author of the long-time bestseller *A Random Walk Down Wall Street*, wrote in *The Wall Street Journal* on April 4, 2000 (p. A24): "To be sure, we know in retrospect that stock prices tend to...revert to the mean. But it's never possible to know in advance when the reversion [to the mean] will occur." William Bernstein expresses the same view in his bestseller, *The Four Pillars of Investing* (p. 231): "You are going to have to live with the markets the way they are—good years and bad years, occurring in a completely unpredictable sequence." You probably have heard that same conventional wisdom from a mutual fund company or financial adviser. This book indicates that the S&P 500 is in fact more predictable than these experts think it to be.

Scientific Test

A scientific test of the WSTL model refutes the contention that the S&P 500 was unpredictable on a short-term basis during 1970-2006. This test is simple. It divided 1935-2006—a total of 72 years—into two periods of about equal length: 1935-1969 (the **sample period**) and 1970-2006 (the **test period**, which academic studies generally call an **out-of-sample period**.). Both periods included many stock market cycles. The WSTL model was developed by incorporating patterns of the S&P 500's *annual returns* and its *short-term movements* during 1935-1969.[2] The sample period begins with 1935 because the WSTL model's yearly forecasts became reliable starting that year. After developing the model, its predictive ability was tested by applying it to 1970-2006. The model's powerful performance for the test period is summarized in the next section.

The 1935-1969 period might seem too long ago to be relevant today. After all, during 1970-2006 there were extensive changes in the tax code [including the creation of 401(k)s and IRAs], massive advances in information technology and major changes in governmental regulatory policies; also, stock trading became dominated by mutual funds and other institutional investors. Furthermore, the U.S. economy was much larger and far more international in scope during the test period. Nevertheless, the following distributions of annual returns for the two periods are remarkably similar.

	Number of Years during	
S&P 500 Annual Return	**1935-1969**	**1970-2006**
Equal to or better than 33.0%	5	3
25.0% to 32.9%	5	6
17.0% to 24.9%	7	8
9.0% to 16.9%	4	5
0.0% to 8.9%	4	7
−0.1% to −8.9%	5	3
Equal to or worse than −9.0%	5	5
Total	35	37

Note: For 1935-2006, the S&P 500's mean annual return was 13.0%.

What the distributions do now show is that the strong force of reversion to the mean was similar in both periods.

The high accuracy rate of forecasting the specific years in which reversion to the mean would occur and would not occur was the primary driver of the WSTL's powerful performance for 1970-2006. Chapter 2 explains the role that the S&P 500's returns reverting to the mean plays in the WSTL model.

Powerful Performance Achieved with Infrequent Trades

Two aspects of an investment's performance are return and risk. **Return** is the change in an investment's value (including reinvested dividends) for a specified period, stated as a percent of its value at the beginning of the period. In this book, all returns are expressed on an *annual basis*. The "Two Components of Return" box explains the important distinction between the S&P 500's *return* and its *price change*.

Two Components of Return

The **S&P 500's return** is the sum of its price change and its reinvested dividends. As an example, consider the year 2006. The **S&P 500's price change** (from 1248.29 at the end of 2005 to 1418.30 at the end of 2006) was 13.6% and the **reinvested dividends** of the companies in the S&P 500 Index were 2.2%. As a result, the S&P 500's return for 2006 was 15.8%.

Risk is the uncertainty regarding the future value of an investment. In the practical application of this definition, investors mainly concern themselves with the possibility of an investment losing money. As an extreme example of risk, the S&P 500 fell 19.3% during a six-week period in the summer of 1998.

Many investors unwisely focus on returns while paying little attention to risk. No investment strategy can be adequately judged without considering returns *and* risk. The WSTL strategy measures both returns and risk. The performance of the WSTL strategy was powerful for 1970-2006 because the WSTL had higher returns with lower risk than buying-and-holding the S&P 500.

- The *compound annual growth rate*—the most comprehensive measure of return, which will be compared to the mean annual return in Chapter 3—was 14.16% for the WSTL versus 11.22% for buy-and-hold. That means the WSTL had 26.2% more return: (14.16% − 11.22%) ÷ 11.22% = 26.2%. The following bar chart compares the pretax growth of a one-time investment of $10,000 at the end of 1969 through the end of 2006 (with dividends and interest reinvested).

It is obvious that the difference in annual growth (14.16% − 11.22% = 2.94 percentage points) had a profound effect when compounded over 1970-2006. There was $830,350 more return from using the WSTL strategy.

- The depth and duration of the S&P 500's downside volatility—a comprehensive measure of risk, which will be explained and calculated in Chapter 4—was 11.6% for the WSTL versus 16.5% for buy-and-hold. Based on that measure, the WSTL had 29.7% less risk: (11.6% − 16.5%) ÷ 16.5% = −29.7%. The following bar chart compares risk as measured by the depth and duration of downside volatility:

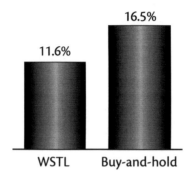

Consider another measure of risk. The S&P 500 had a negative return for eight of the years during 1970-2006. *The WSTL had a higher return for every one of those years.* That is, the WSTL model had a successful trade out of and back into the S&P 500 in each of the eight years.

Chapter 4 discusses the two measures of risk above along with six others. *All eight of them favor the WSTL.* That's the important sleep-well aspect of the WSTL strategy.

- In achieving higher returns with lower risk for 1970-2006, the WSTL strategy had an average of one (round-trip) trade—out of the S&P 500 in the early part of the year and back into the S&P 500 later in the year—every three years. Of the 13 trades during that period, 11 were profitable. Chapter 2 provides details on those trades.

A **profitable trade** means that, for the period when the WSTL is red, the S&P 500 return is less than the interest the WSTL investor earns on 3-month T-bills or in a money market fund. Consequently, the WSTL return is greater than the S&P 500 return for the year in which a profitable trade occurs. In some years, a profitable trade means that the WSTL has a smaller negative return than the S&P 500. As an example, a profitable trade amounting to 9.5% occurred in 2002. For that year the WSTL return was −12.6% while the S&P 500 return was −22.1%. Each of the profitable trades occurred primarily because the S&P 500 had a sizable fall for the period in which the WSTL was red. In 2002, the S&P 500 fell nearly 11.0% for the 4.7 months that the WSTL was red.

An **unprofitable trade** means that, for the period when the WSTL is red, the S&P 500 return is greater than the interest the WSTL investor earns on 3-month T-bills or in a money market fund. Consequently, the WSTL return is less than the S&P 500 return for the year in which an unprofitable trade occurs. For example, an unprofitable trade amounting to −5.1% occurred in 2005. For that year the WSTL return was −0.2% while the S&P 500 return was 4.9%. Each of the unprofitable trades occurred primarily because the S&P 500 rose for the period in which the WSTL was red. In 2005, the S&P 500 rose 5.8% for the 10.0 months that the WSTL was red.

Having an occasional unprofitable trade need not be disastrous. To that point, Ken Fisher, a long-time *Forbes* columnist and renowned money manager, observed that: "Getting defensive successfully, even if you don't do it perfectly, can provide you a major and lasting performance boost."[3] The WSTL strategy's trades during 1970-2006 demonstrate the wisdom of Fisher's observation.

It is widely believed today that past stock prices (or any other data) are not useful in making yearly forecasts which, over the long-term, achieve higher returns with lower risk compared to buy-and-hold. Although past performance is no guarantee of future results, the WSTL strategy's market-beating performance for 1970-2006 resulting from infrequent market timing strongly contradicts that conventional wisdom.

Expert Opinions

In general, practitioners and academicians in the investment community believe that market timing—such as the WSTL strategy uses—is a fool's errand. Here is how four Wall Street legends expressed that belief:

- In the 1992 annual report of Berkshire Hathaway Corporation, Warren Buffett stated: "We've long felt that the only value of stock forecasters is to make fortune tellers look good.... Short-term market forecasts are poison and should be kept locked up in a safe place, away from children and also from grown-ups who behave in the market like children."

- John Bogle, founder and former chairman of The Vanguard Group, said: "After nearly fifty years in this business, I do not know of anybody who has done it [market timing] successfully and consistently. I don't even know anybody who *knows* anybody who has done it successfully and consistently."[4]

- Peter Lynch, the top-performing mutual fund manager of all time, said: "I've sat...through some of the most terrible [stock market] drops, and I couldn't have figured them out beforehand if my life had depended on it."[5]

- Benjamin Graham, the father of security analysis, said: "If I have noticed anything over these 60 years on Wall Street, it is that people do not succeed in forecasting what's going to happen in the stock market."[6]

You will not find an endorsement there for any market-timing strategy! But in this book, history relating to the WSTL model speaks for itself. Read on and you will find it is certainly educational and potentially beneficial for the future performance of your 401(k)/IRA.

Alpha

The difference between the performance of a professional money manager (or a market-timing model such as the WSTL) and the performance of an appropriate **benchmark** (such as the S&P 500) is called **alpha**. To calculate a market-timing model's alpha, the compound annual growth rate (CAGR) that it produced is adjusted for risk and reduced by its annual investment costs. Earlier in this chapter, you saw that the CAGR for 1970-2006 was 2.94 percentage points higher for the WSTL than buying-and-holding the S&P 500. In recent years, it cost only 0.12% a year to own a low-cost S&P 500 index fund; reducing the 2.94 by 0.12 leaves 2.82 percentage points. Since the risk of the WSTL model was lower than buy-and-hold's risk for 1970-2006, that means, after adjusting for risk, the WSTL's alpha actually was *greater than* 2.82 *percentage points*. That is an impressive alpha.

What generated the WSTL's alpha? It was either a well-thought-out investment philosophy that is credible or luck or some combination of those two possibilities. The WSTL model makes a forecast each year of precisely when the S&P 500 will move higher or precisely when it will move lower. About once every three years during 1970-2006, a forecast resulted in a "sell" signal (a signal to sell the S&P 500) and then a "buy" signal (a signal to buy back the S&P 500). *The high degree of accuracy of those signals is what generated the WSTL's alpha.* The large number of accurate forecasts produced by the WSTL model for 1970-2006 (37 years) essentially eliminates the possibility that those forecasts were due to luck. In other words, the WSTL proved itself to be a well-thought-out investment philosophy that is credible.

If indeed the WSTL strategy is well-conceived, there is real potential for you to generate an enviable alpha in your 401(k)/IRA by merely acting on the signals as they occur in the future. The yearly forecasts of the S&P 500's short-term movement described in the next chapter provide the precise timing of those signals.

Simple to Understand and Use

Each trading day a tidal wave of numbers flows from the stock market—prices of individual stocks, numerous indices, trading volume, earnings per share, price/earnings ratios and so on. Amidst this mind-numbing sea of numbers, the WSTL model—in the purest form of technical analysis—is based on *two series of numbers: the S&P 500's annual returns and its daily closing prices.* In other words, the color of the WSTL at any particular time is entirely a function of *what the S&P 500 did in the recent past.* Consequently, the WSTL model is *simple to understand* in the sense that *no knowledge is required of the economic, geopolitical and market factors which moved the S&P 500 in the past or will move it in the future.* From the standpoint of acting on the WSTL buy and sell signals, that means you can ignore news items regarding the actions of the Federal Reserve, corporate earnings, oil prices, the yield curve, the federal deficit, the value of the U.S. dollar relative to foreign currencies, subprime mortgages and the like.

Even for the well-informed individual investor, explaining the economic, geopolitical and market reasons for the S&P 500's movements can be confusing and frustrating. The same is true for professional money managers, market strategists, financial advisers and financial journalists. As a recent example, it was stated on the front page of *The Wall Street Journal* on August 14, 2007, that: "In the past month, the market has been behaving in ways even seasoned players have been at a loss to explain."

The confusion and frustration exists because the S&P 500's movements (and stock markets around the world) tend not to be intuitive. Economic and geopolitical news often affects the S&P 500 in different ways, at different times and in different economic cycles. When investors feel upbeat, they focus on the news that supports a rosy outlook. If sentiment is negative, they see the glass half-empty and look for cracks.[7] Meanwhile, *the WSTL regards the S&P 500's annual returns and its daily closing prices as the news.*

As an illustration of the distinction between "what the S&P 500 did" versus "the economic reasons why the S&P 500 did what it did," consider the day I am writing this paragraph (May 18, 2007). *The Wall Street Journal* reported this news item (released yesterday): U.S. building permits had their biggest decline in nearly 17 years, raising the prospect that the housing market will remain weak. Yesterday regular unleaded gasoline was selling for $3.19 a gallon, an all-time high where I live (Tulsa, Oklahoma). Isn't it the most obvious implication that paying more for gasoline will reduce consumer spending on all other things and hurt the economy? However, yesterday the S&P 500 closed within 1.0% of its all-time high, set on March 24, 2000. Based on the very limited contents of this paragraph, there obviously is a major disconnect between what the S&P 500 did and the economic reasons why it did what it did.

Now consider the forecasting perspective. Market participants and market commentators often forecast the direction of the S&P 500 based on their interpretation of economic trends. For example, a commentator may say, "the inflation rate is increasing and will continue to increase, so the Fed will raise interest rates and the S&P 500 will be hard-pressed to maintain its upward momentum." Or, "the overheated Chinese stock market is going to have a fall soon, which will result in a headwind for stocks around the world." Or, "the current level of the S&P 500 is supported by strong fundamentals, so a rise will begin soon." Since such forecasts have had a strong tendency to be off the mark, the commentary accompanying most of them is really only intellectual sport.

Several reasons explain why it is *simple to use* the WSTL strategy in your 401(k)/IRA:

- My estimate is that less than 10 hours a year is needed to use the strategy. If you do nothing more than monitor the color changes at thewallstreettrafficlight.com, my estimate drops to less than five hours a year.

- Quarterly performance updates and brief monthly commentaries, beginning in January 2008, are available at thewallstreettrafficlight.com.

- The strategy utilizes two investment vehicles: a low-cost S&P 500 index fund and a money market fund. Chapter 6 recommends Fidelity's Spartan 500 Index Fund and Vanguard's 500 Index Fund as well as two exchange-traded (ETF) S&P 500 index funds, "Spiders" and iShares S&P 500 Index Fund. Using any of these recommended funds, *you can invest each multiple of $10,000 for less than 3½¢ a day.* What a bargain!

- Executing both halves of a round-trip trade out of and back into an S&P 500 index fund requires only a few minutes.

Using Common Sense

John Bogle offered this sage advice for choosing an appropriate investment strategy: "Although there is no guarantee that...patterns of the past, no matter how deeply ingrained in the historical record, will prevail in the future, a study of the past, accompanied by a self-administered dose of common sense, is the intelligent investor's best recourse."[8] After reading this book, and perhaps after monitoring the WSTL's future performance for a while, you can decide if this strategy passes your common-sense test.

Chapter 2

◇◇◇◇◇◇◇◇◇◇◇◇◇◇

YEARLY FORECASTS OF THE S&P 500

Power Points

1. Seven types of years classified in the WSTL model: 1A, 1B, 1C, Tier 2, 3A, 3B and 3C. The yearly forecasts of the S&P 500—either "will exceed the long-term mean" or "will move lower"—are linked to the seven types of years.

2. There are no trades in 1A, Tier 2 and 3A years. For each of those types of years, the WSTL stays green throughout the year.

3. There is a trade in each 1B, 1C, 3B and 3C year. For each of those types of years, the WSTL is green at the beginning of the year, turns red on a particular day between the end of January and the end of April, and then turns green and stays that color for the remainder of the year.

4. For two of the 13 years that had trades during 1970-2006, the day of the buy signal—when the WSTL turned from red to green—was the S&P 500's low for the year.

5. The WSTL was red approximately 20% of the time during 1970-2006. The generally poor performance of the S&P 500 when the WSTL was red was the primary driver of the WSTL strategy beating buy-and-hold.

Each yearly forecast of the S&P 500 was either "will exceed the long-term mean" or "will move lower." The WSTL's powerful performance for 1970-2006 was attributable to the high accuracy rate of those forecasts.

This chapter provides the specifications for making the yearly forecasts of the S&P 500. If you prefer not to involve yourself in the details, keep in mind that the forecasts manifest themselves in a simple way: the WSTL is either green or red at any given time. You can monitor the color of the WSTL anytime by going to thewallstreettrafficlight.com. Also available at the site are brief monthly commentaries, which indicate when the color is close to changing and the exact day when it does change.

Because this chapter is packed with information, it is divided into two main sections: (1) the seven types of years and (2) the forecasts and outcomes for 1970-2006. Read each section in a separate sitting, if you prefer.

THE SEVEN TYPES OF YEARS

The core of the WSTL model is a "type-of-year" framework. Under the framework, seven types of years are classified into what I call Tier 1, Tier 2 and Tier 3. Each **tier** specifies *a range for the S&P 500's mean return for the two-year period immediately preceding the year being classified*. **Tier 1** is the *upper range* for two-year mean returns, **Tier 2** is the *middle range* and **Tier 3** is the *lower range*. The specifications for the years in the three tiers are set forth later in this chapter.

Six of the seven types of years—all years except those in Tier 2—are classified into three categories based on the S&P 500's movement in the early months of the year being classified. I call them category A, category B and category C. Each **category** specifies a set of *conditions for the S&P 500's movement, during part or all of the January-through-April period, in relation to its December low of the prior year*. The specifications for the A, B and C categories are set forth later in the chapter.

Exhibit 2-1 lists the seven types of years. Except for years in Tier 2 (which do not involve categories A, B or C), all other types of years are a combination of a tier and a category.

Exhibit 2-1

WSTL Model's Seven Types of Years

Tier	Category	Type of Year
1	A	1A
1	B	1B
1	C	1C
2	Not applicable	Tier 2
3	A	3A
3	B	3B
3	C	3C

The **type of year** determines the forecast of the S&P 500 for that year as follows:

Type of Year	Forecast of the S&P 500
1A	Will exceed the long-term mean
1B	Will move lower
1C	Will move lower
Tier 2	Will exceed the long-term mean
3A	Will exceed the long-term mean
3B	Will move lower
3C	Will move lower

Based on the "will exceed the long-term mean" forecast for the **1A**, Tier 2 and **3A** years, the WSTL is green throughout those years. The "will move lower" forecast for the **1B**, **1C**, **3B** and **3C** years is predicting that there will be enough of a downside move in the S&P 500 to produce a profitable trade. As a result, the WSTL is red during part of those years.

Specifications for Years in Tier 1, Tier 2 and Tier 3

To classify any given year into one of the three tiers, the WSTL model focuses on the two-year period immediately before it. That is, 1933-34 preceded 1935, 1934-35 preceded 1936...and 2004-05 preceded 2006. The tiers are based on the S&P 500's mean annual return for the two-year period immediately preceding the year being classified. For example, the S&P 500's returns for 1997 and 1998 were 33.4% and 28.6%, respectively; that two-year mean was 31.0%.

The following specifications for the three tiers were developed for 1935-1969 (explained in Chapter 9), then were applied to 1970-2006 and will be applied to the years after the publication of this book in 2007:

Tier	S&P 500's Two-Year Mean Annual Return Immediately Preceding the Year Being Classified	That Two-Year Mean Annual Return in Relation to the S&P 500's Long-Term of 13.0%
1	Above 13.6%	Above
2	6.2% to 13.6%	Below to slightly above
3	Below 6.2%	Farther below

Note that each year would be classified into a particular tier *before the year began.* That's because the S&P 500's mean annual return for the preceding two-year period would be known by the end of December immediately preceding the year being classified. For example, since the S&P 500's average annual return for 1970-71 was 9.2% [(the sum of the 4.0% return for 1970 and the 14.3% return for 1971) ÷ 2 = 9.2%], 1972 would be classified into Tier 2 immediately before that year began.

The S&P 500 had a strong tendency to generate returns above the long-term mean of 13.0% for the years in Tier 2 during 1935-1969. As a result, the model specified that the WSTL is green throughout each Tier 2 year during 1970-2006.

Specifications for Years in the A, B and C Categories

According to an old adage, it is not how something starts but how it finishes that matters. For example, a football team might fall behind two touchdowns in the first half but rally to win the game. The wisdom of this adage, however, does *not* describe the movements of the S&P 500 in most years during 1935-1969 and 1970-2006. In fact, history indicates that *the S&P 500's movement during the early months of the calendar year, in relation to its December low of the prior year, tended to set the tone for the year as a whole.*

A specific set of conditions for the WSTL model was used to classify each Tier 1 and Tier 3 year during 1970-2006 into category A, B or C.

Category "A" year. This classification occurs when the S&P 500 meets *either of the following conditions:*

1. The lowest daily closing price during the prior year's December (the December low) was "not broken" during the January-through-April period of the year being classified, meaning that none of the S&P 500's daily closing prices during the January-through-April period were lower than the December low. (Note that under this condition it does not matter whether January's price change was positive or negative.)

   or

2. The prior year's December low was broken during January (but was not broken during the February-through-April period) of the year being classified, *and* January's price change was positive.

The classification of a category "A" year is established *at the end of April.*

During 1935-1969, the S&P 500 had a strong tendency to produce above-average returns for the years in Tier 1 and Tier 3 that were in category "A" (that is, 1A and 3A years). As a result, the model specifies that the WSTL is green throughout each 1A and 3A year after 1969.

Category "B" year. This classification occurs when the S&P 500 meets *both of the following conditions:*

1. The prior year's December low was broken during the February-through-April period of the year being classified. (It does not matter whether the December low was broken during January.)

   and

2. January's price change was positive.

The classification of a category "B" year is established *on a particular day during the February-through-April period*. That day is the "sell" signal, the day when the WSTL turns from green to red.

During 1935-1969, the S&P 500 had a strong tendency to have poor performance, at least early in the year, for the years in Tier 1 and Tier 3 that were in category "B" (that is, 1B and 3B years). As a result, the model specifies that the WSTL, which is always green for the entire month of January, turns red on a particular day between the beginning of February and the end of April in each 1B and 3B year after 1969. Later in the year, the WSTL turns green on the day of the "buy" signal and stays that color for the remainder of the year. The model specifies that the latest time the WSTL could turn from red to green in a 1B or 3B year is the end of September.

Category "C" year. This classification occurs when the S&P 500 meets *both of the following conditions:*

1. The prior year's December low was broken during the January-through-April period of the year being classified.

    and

2. January's price change was negative.

The classification of a category "C" year is established *on a particular day between the end of January and the end of April*. That day is the sell signal, the day when the WSTL turns from green to red.

During 1935-1969, the S&P 500 had a strong tendency to have poor performance, at least early in the year, for the years in Tier 1 and Tier 3 that were in the "C" category (that is 1C and 3C years). As a result, the model specifies that the WSTL, which is always green for the entire month of January, turns red on a particular day between the end of January and the end of April in each 1C and 3C year after 1969. Later in the year, the WSTL turns green and stays that color for the remainder of the year. The model specifies that the latest time the WSTL could turn from red to green in a 1C or 3C year is the end of November.

The Prior Year's December Low. The conditions that define category A, B and C years refer to the S&P 500's prior year's December low. Since December is the end of the tax year, considerable tax-related selling occurs at that time. Two situations trigger tax-related selling. First, investors sell stocks to take ("realize") losses that either will be offset against capital gains they realized earlier in the year or otherwise are deductible for tax purposes. Second, investors sell stocks to realize gains that will be offset against capital losses they realized earlier in the year or in prior years.

It is intuitive that some (perhaps even a high proportion of) tax-related selling in the S&P 500 stocks has *nothing* to do with their investment worthiness per se. Consequently, those stock prices would be temporarily depressed by tax-related selling during December. All other things being equal, this selling pressure will ease by the turn of the calendar year and likely will stimulate some buying of (that is, "bargain hunting" in) those same stocks in January. In the absence of investors' pessimism during the January-through-April period, history has shown that the prior year's December low will be durable (that is, it will not be broken). On the other hand, if investors are pessimistic in the early months of the year, history has shown that it is highly likely that the prior year's December low will be broken—despite bargain hunting in January.

Flowchart. Exhibit 2-2 consolidates the conditions for years in categories A, B and C into a flowchart. The flowchart consists of three questions (symbolized by diamonds) and four conclusions (ovals) designating the type of year. Having four conclusions but only three types of years is attributable to the fact that a category "A" year occurs when *either* of two conditions is met, whereas category "B" and "C" years each occur only one way—when *both* of their respective conditions are met.

Exhibit 2-2

Flowchart for Classifying Years into the A, B and C Categories

The question in each diamond refers to a movement of the S&P 500.

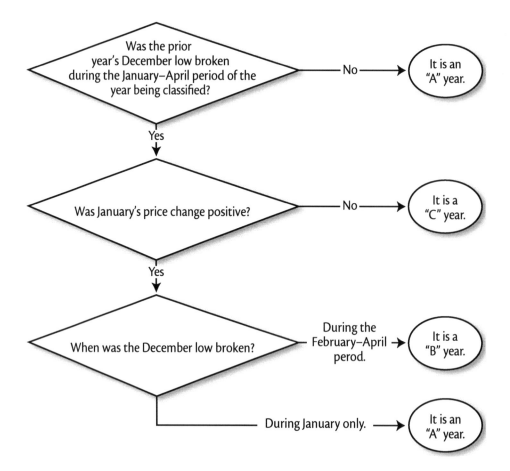

The first question in the flowchart is answered as follows: Until the A, B or C category is established during the January 31st-through-April 30th period, compare the S&P 500's daily closing price to the prior year's December low. (The work is done for you at thewallstreettrafficlight.com.) If the December low was not broken by the end of April, the year is in category "A."

If the December low was broken by the end of April, the second question in the flowchart is answered by comparing January's closing price to the prior December's closing price. If January's price change was negative, the year is in category "C," with that classification established on the day the December low was broken or at the end of January (whichever occurs later). If January's price change was positive, the final question is, *when was the December low broken?* If the break came during the February-through-April period, the year is in category "B," with that classification established on the day of the break. If the break came during January only, the year is in category "A," with that classification established at the end of April. Note that *no calculations are needed to answer any of the questions in the flowchart.*

THE FORECASTS AND OUTCOMES FOR 1970-2006

Since the WSTL is always green for the entire month of January, that means each year begins on an optimistic note. The optimism is warranted because the S&P 500's mean return for January was 0.9% for 1935-1969 and 1.6% for 1970-2006.

Earlier in this chapter, it was stated that each year's forecast of the S&P 500 depends on which type of year it is. Let's review the forecast for a 1A year. Being in Tier 1, the year had a mean annual return for the preceding two years that was above 13.6%. Being in category "A," the S&P 500 moved higher for the January-through-April period. The 1A year's forecast for the S&P 500 is "will exceed the long-term mean" (that is, will exceed 13.0%). As a result, the WSTL stays green throughout the year.

Now let's shift our focus and use *reversion to the mean* as the basis to make the forecast for a 1A year. In that case, the forecast for the S&P 500 is "will not revert downward" in relation to its long-term mean. Exhibit 2-3 indicates the forecast of the S&P 500 in relation to its long-term mean for each type of year. Based on those forecasts, a trade is made out of the S&P 500 and then back into it in each 1B, 1C, 3B and 3C year.

Exhibit 2-3

Summary of the WSTL Model

For each type of year in bold, a trade is made out of and then back into a low-cost S&P 500 index fund.

Type of Year	Forecast of the S&P 500 in Relation to Its Long-Term Mean	When Forecast Is Made	Color Pattern of WSTL during the Year
1A	Will not revert downward	April 30th	Green throughout
1B	Will revert downward	February 1st to April 30th*	Green, then red, then green
1C	Will revert downward	January 31st to April 30th*	Green, then red, then green
Tier 2	Will revert upward	Immediately before the year begins	Green throughout
3A	Will revert upward	April 30th	Green throughout
3B	Will not revert upward	February 1st to April 30th*	Green, then red, then green
3C	Will not revert upward	January 31st to April 30th*	Green, then red, then green

*On a particular day during that period.

This exhibit is comprehensive. Review it carefully before proceeding.

Trades for 1970-2006

Each WSTL (round-trip) trade is executed in the following manner. On the day of the sell signal (the day the classification of a year in category B or C is established), the S&P 500 is sold and the proceeds are put into 3-month Treasury bills. Then, on the day of the buy signal, the S&P 500 is bought with the funds accumulated in the T-bills. The WSTL is red for the period from the sell signal to the buy signal. The WSTL investor's watchword in 1B, 1C, 3B and 3C years after 2006 is "sell a low-cost S&P 500 index fund in his 401(k)/IRA and buy it back at a lower price."

Historically, the WSTL strategy invested in 3-month T-bills while the WSTL was red. That essentially risk-free investment was used because of its availability throughout 1935-2006. Money market funds, which also are essentially risk-free, did not become available to individual investors until the late 1970s. The rate on 3-month T-bills has tended to be slightly less than the rate on money market funds. Note that for convenience, after 2006 the WSTL strategy will use a money market fund instead of 3-month T-bills.

Be aware that the WSTL strategy receives no S&P 500 dividends while the WSTL is red. That point is important because reinvested dividends accounted for slightly more than 29% of the S&P 500's mean return for 1970-2006. The other 71% of the return was attributable to the S&P 500's price increase.

Let's look at the 13 trades during 1970-2006—an average of one trade every three years. Exhibit 2-4 summarizes the outcomes of those trades. The average (mean) profit per trade was 7.1%. Eleven of the trades were "profitable," which means the WSTL return was higher than the S&P 500 return for each of those years. Likewise in the case of the two "unprofitable" trades, the WSTL return was lower than the S&P 500 return for each of those years. Note that, even though the profit on the trade in 1973 amounted to *11.7%*, the WSTL return itself for that year was −3.0%. In other words, the WSTL strategy decisively beat the S&P 500 for 1973, but lost a small amount of money that year.

Exhibit 2-4

The Thirteen Trades, 1970-2006

Year	Type of Year	WSTL Return	S&P 500 Return	Outcome of Trade
1970	3C	17.7%	4.0%	13.7%
1973	1C	−3.0%	−14.7%	11.7%
1974	3C	−16.0%	−26.5%	10.5%
1977	1C	4.5%	−7.2%	1.7%
1981	1C	13.1%	−4.9%	18.0%
1982	1C	39.8%	21.4%	18.4%
1984	1C	8.7%	6.3%	2.4%
1990	1C	2.1%	−3.2%	5.2%*
2000	1C	0.1%	−9.1%	9.2%
2001	3B	−6.3%	−11.9%	5.6%
2002	3C	−12.6%	−22.1%	9.5%
2003	3C	10.3%	28.7%	−18.4%
2005	1C	−0.2%	4.9%	−5.1%
Mean		4.5%	−2.6%	7.1%

*This difference does not add across due to rounding.

The main driver of the profitable trades in the exhibit is the S&P 500 had a sizable fall for the period in which the WSTL was red. The two unprofitable trades during 1970-2006 saw the S&P 500 rise for the period in which the WSTL was red. Chapter 10 explains the detailed calculations necessary to determine the WSTL return for each of the years in the exhibit.

In the last column of the exhibit are 11 consecutive profitable trades followed by two unprofitable ones. Is it significant that the pattern went from success to failure? I do not think so; the pattern simply indicates it is unlikely that *all* WSTL trades will be profitable in the future. While two successive unprofitable trades would have been an unpleasant experience, they should be considered in the context of the WSTL model's outstanding long-term performance.

A Close Look at Selected Buy Signals

Following the sell signal in each 1B, 1C, 3B and 3C year, the buy signal occurs later in the year—at which time the WSTL turns from red to green.[9] The WSTL model was built so that it is possible for the buy signal to occur *on or near the day of the S&P 500's lowest closing price during the year.* The following table indicates that outcome did happen for three of the 13 buy signals during 1970-2006:

Year	Type of Year	Buy Signal	Year's Low	Trading Days from Buy Signal to Year's Low
1970	3C	05/14/70	05/26/70	8
1977	1C	11/02/77	11/02/77	0
1981	1C	09/25/81	09/25/81	0

The timing of those buy signals is extraordinary, which helps to explain why the WSTL strategy achieved higher returns with lower risk than buying-and-holding the S&P 500 for 1970-2006.

The Big Picture

Exhibit 2-5 displays the big picture of the large amount of material presented in this chapter for 1970-2006. Focus on four main points in the exhibit. First, each "x" in the exhibit represents approximately a one-week period when the WSTL was red. Those weeks accounted for about 20% of the total time during 1970-2006. Second, when the WSTL was green throughout the year (that is, a 1A, Tier 2 or 3A year), the WSTL return was the same as the S&P 500 return; see the two return columns near the right side of the exhibit. Third, when the WSTL was red in a year, the WSTL return for that year differed from the S&P 500 return, due to the outcome of the trade; see the last column in the exhibit. Fourth, the compound annual growth rate (at the bottom of the exhibit) was 14.16% for the WSTL versus 11.22% for buy-and-hold. The next chapter calculates those rates and illustrates that the difference between them, 2.94 percentage points, is large when expressed in dollar terms over the 1970-2006 period.

Exhibit 2-5

The Big Picture for 1970-2006

Each "x" represents approximately one week when the WSTL was red.

Year	Type of Year	Jan	Feb	Mar	Apr	May	Jun	Jul	Aug	Sep	Oct	Nov	Dec	WSTL Return	S&P 500 Return	Outcome of Trade
1970	3C		xxxx	xxxx	xxxx	xx								17.7%	4.0%	13.7%
1971	3A													14.3%	14.3%	
1972	Tier 2													19.0%	19.0%	
1973	1C		xxxx	xxxx	xxxx	xxxx	xxxx	x						−3.0%	−14.7%	11.7%
1974	3C		xxx	xxxx	xxxx	xxxx	xxxx	xx						−16.0%	−26.5%	10.5%
1975	3A													37.2%	37.2%	
1976	3A													23.8%	23.8%	
1977	1C		xxxx	xxxx	xxxx	xxxx	xxxx	xxxx	xxxx	xxxx	xxxx	x		4.5%	−7.2%	11.7%
1978	Tier 2													6.6%	6.6%	
1979	3A													18.4%	18.4%	
1980	Tier 2													32.4%	32.4%	
1981	1C		xxxx	xxxx	xxxx	xxxx	xxxx	xxxx	xxxx	xxxx				13.1%	−4.9%	18.0%
1982	1C		xxxx	xxxx	xxxx	xxxx	xxx							39.8%	21.4%	18.4%
1983	Tier 2													22.5%	22.5%	
1984	1C		xxxx	xxxx	xxxx	xxxx	xxxx	xxxx	xxxx	xxxx	xxxx	xxxx		8.7%	6.3%	2.4%
1985	1A													32.2%	32.2%	
1986	1A													18.5%	18.5%	
1987	1A													5.2%	5.2%	
1988	Tier 2													16.8%	16.8%	
1989	Tier 2													31.5%	31.5%	
1990	1C		xxxx	xxxx	xxxx	xxxx	xxxx	xxxx	xxxx	xxxx	xxxx	xxxx		2.1%	−3.2%	5.2%*
1991	1A													30.6%	30.6%	
1992	1A													7.7%	7.7%	
1993	1A													10.0%	10.0%	
1994	Tier 2													1.3%	1.3%	
1995	3A													37.4%	37.4%	
1996	1A													23.1%	23.1%	
1997	1A													33.4%	33.4%	
1998	1A													28.6%	28.6%	
1999	1A													21.0%	21.0%	
2000	1C		xxxx	xxxx	xxxx	xxxx	xxxx	xxxx	xxxx	xxxx	xxxx	xxxx		0.1%	−9.1%	9.2%
2001	3B		x	xx										−6.3%	−11.9%	5.6%
2002	3C		xxxx	xxxx	xxxx	xxxx	xxx							−12.6%	−22.1%	9.5%
2003	3C		xxxx	xxxx	xxxx	xxxx	xx							10.3%	28.7%	−18.4%
2004	3A													10.9%	10.9%	
2005	1C		xxxx	xxxx	xxxx	xxxx	xxxx	xxxx	xxxx	xxxx	xxxx	xxxx		−0.2%	4.9%	−5.1%
2006	Tier 2													15.8%	15.8%	
Compound annual growth rate														14.16%	11.22%	

*This difference does not add across due to rounding.

Dow Trifectas

It is interesting to end this chapter by looking at a phenomenon I call a Dow trifecta. A **Dow trifecta** occurs when three Dow Jones averages—the Industrials, the Transports and the Utilities—all hit an all-time high on the same day. There have been Dow trifectas in six different years during 1935-2006. Five of those years—1985, 1986, 1987, 1993, and 1998—were 1A years. For a 1A year, the forecast of the S&P 500's movement in relation to its long-term mean of 13.0% was "will not revert downward." The sixth year that had a Dow trifecta, 1964, was a Tier 2 year. For a Tier 2 year, the forecast of the S&P 500's movement in relation to its long-term mean is "will revert upward."

Since each of the six years that had Dow trifectas was classified as either a 1A or Tier 2 year, the WSTL was green throughout those years. The S&P 500's mean return for the six Dow-trifecta years was 18.5%—an impressive 5.5 percentage points greater than its long-term mean.

Chapter 3

◇◇◇◇◇◇◇◇◇◇◇◇◇◇◇◇◇

ANNUAL RETURNS AND CAGR
FOR 1970-2006

Power Points

1. The S&P 500's mean annual return was 22.0% for the sixteen 1A and 3A years during 1970-2006. That is 9.5 percentage points greater than the S&P 500's mean return for all years during 1970-2006. None of the 1A or 3A years had a negative return.

2. The S&P 500's mean annual return was 18.2% for the eight Tier 2 years during 1970-2006. None of those years had a negative return.

3. For 1970-2006, the WSTL's compound annual growth rate (CAGR) was 14.16% versus 11.22% for buy-and-hold. As a result, a one-time investment of $10,000 at the end of 1969 grew to $1,342,527 at the end of 2006 under the WSTL strategy versus $512,179 under buy-and-hold.

The first section of this chapter focuses on the annual returns for the 1A, 3A and Tier 2 years during 1970-2006. Since there were no trades in those years, the returns for the WSTL and the S&P 500 are the same (that is, the WSTL was green throughout each of those years). It was highly desirable to be invested in the S&P 500 in the 1A, 3A and Tier 2 years because their mean annual return was 20.7%, which was 8.2 percentage points greater than the mean return for all years during 1970-2006.

This chapter explains why the compound annual growth rate (CAGR) is better than the mean to measure an investment strategy's return. CAGR is calculated for the WSTL strategy and for buying-and-holding the S&P 500 for 1970-2006.

Returns for 1A, 3A and Tier 2 Years

Of the 37 years comprising 1970-2006, ten were 1A years and six were 3A years; that is 43.2% of the years in that period. Exhibit 3-1 presents the returns for those years, ranked from best to worst. Their mean return was 22.0%, which is 9.5 percentage points greater than the mean return of 12.5% for all years during 1970-2006. The mean return for 1A years and for 3A years was similar—21.0% and 23.7%, respectively. Five of the years in the exhibit had returns of at least 30.6%. Only two years had returns of less than 10.0%; the lowest return was 5.2% for 1987.

Exhibit 3-1

Returns for the 1A and 3A Years, 1970-2006

For these years, the WSTL return is the same as the S&P 500 return.

Year	Type of Year	Return (ranked best to worst)
1995	3A	37.4%
1975	3A	37.2%
1997	1A	33.4%
1985	1A	32.2%
1991	1A	30.6%
1998	1A	28.6%
1976	3A	23.8%
1996	1A	23.1%
1999	1A	21.0%
1986	1A	18.5%
1979	3A	18.4%
1971	3A	14.3%
2004	3A	10.9%
1993	1A	10.0%
1992	1A	7.7%
1987	1A	5.2%
Mean		22.0%

During 1970-2006, there were seven Tier 2 years (18.9% of the years in that period). Exhibit 3-2 presents the returns for those years, ranked from best to worst. The mean return for the Tier 2 years was 18.2%, which is 5.7 percentage points greater than the mean return for all years during 1970-2006. Two of the years in the exhibit had returns of at least 31.5% while two years had returns of less than 16.8%. The lowest return among Tier 2 years was 1.3% for 1994.

Exhibit 3-2

Returns for the Tier 2 Years, 1970-2006

For these years, the WSTL return is the same as the S&P 500 return.

Year	Return (ranked best to worst)
1980	32.4%
1989	31.5%
1983	22.5%
1972	19.0%
1988	16.8%
2006	15.8%
1978	6.6%
1994	1.3%
Mean	18.2%

An important implication of Exhibits 3-1 and 3-2 is that *the WSTL strategy avoided the emotional and financial pain market timers would have experienced had they not held the S&P 500 throughout the 1A, 3A and Tier 2 years.* The misery for market timers is to be under-invested in the stock market in any year that had a stellar return.

One-Time Investments by You and Your Neighbor

Consider this example. Suppose you invested $10,000 at the end of 1969 and used the WSTL strategy through the end of 2006. Your neighbor also made a $10,000 investment, but she bought-and-held the S&P 500 for that same period. Although 401(k)s and IRAs had not been created in the early years of the test period, assume that they existed throughout 1970-2006 to modernize this example, and assume that you and your neighbor each put your $10,000 investment in one of those tax-advantaged accounts. Also assume that you reinvested dividends and interest and she reinvested dividends. Finally, assume that neither of you incurred any investment costs. (Chapter 6 will explain that the total investment costs of a low-cost S&P 500 index fund are not more than 0.12% per year, which means it costs less than 3½¢ a day to invest $10,000.)

Exhibit 3-3 presents the dramatic difference between how you and your neighbor fared under the respective investment strategies for 1970-2006. The returns for the 1A, 3A and Tier 2 years are from the first two exhibits in this chapter. The returns for the 1B, 1C, 3B and 3C years—the years that had trades—are from Exhibit 2-4 (p. 21). The shaded total-accumulation figures near the bottom of Exhibit 3-3 indicate that you amassed $1,342,527 while your neighbor amassed only $512,177. That is, your total accumulation was 162% greater than hers: ($1,342,527 − $512,177) ÷ $512,177 = 162%. The bar chart (p. 7) is a summary presentation of the total accumulations in Exhibit 3-3.

Exhibit 3-3

Annual Returns and Total Accumulations for 1970-2006

Year	Type of Year	WSTL Return	End-of-Year Accumulation from One-Time Investment of $10,000 Using the WSTL	S&P 500 Return	End-of-Year Accumulation from One-Time Investment of $10,000 in the S&P 500
1969			$10,000		$10,000
1970	3C	17.7%	$11,770	4.0%	$10,400
1971	3A	14.3%	$13,453	14.3%	$11,887
1972	Tier 2	19.0%	$16,009	19.0%	$14,146
1973	1C	−3.0%	$15,529	−14.7%	$12,066
1974	3C	−16.0%	$13,044	−26.5%	$8,869
1975	3A	37.2%	$17,897	37.2%	$12,168
1976	3A	23.8%	$22,156	23.8%	$15,064
1977	1C	4.5%	$23,153	−7.2%	$13,979
1978	Tier 2	6.6%	$24,681	6.6%	$14,902
1979	3A	18.4%	$29,223	18.4%	$17,644
1980	Tier 2	32.4%	$38,691	32.4%	$23,361
1981	1C	13.1%	$43,759	−4.9%	$22,216
1982	1C	39.8%	$61,176	21.4%	$26,970
1983	Tier 2	22.5%	$74,940	22.5%	$33,038
1984	1C	8.7%	$81,460	6.3%	$35,120
1985	1A	32.2%	$107,690	32.2%	$46,428
1986	1A	18.5%	$127,613	18.5%	$55,018
1987	1A	5.2%	$134,249	5.2%	$57,878
1988	Tier 2	16.8%	$156,802	16.8%	$67,602
1989	Tier 2	31.5%	$206,195	31.5%	$88,897
1990	1C	2.1%	$210,525	−3.2%	$86,052
1991	1A	30.6%	$274,946	30.6%	$112,384
1992	1A	7.7%	$296,117	7.7%	$121,037
1993	1A	10.0%	$325,728	10.0%	$133,141
1994	Tier 2	1.3%	$329,963	1.3%	$134,872
1995	3A	37.4%	$453,369	37.4%	$185,314
1996	1A	23.1%	$558,097	23.1%	$228,122
1997	1A	33.4%	$744,501	33.4%	$304,314
1998	1A	28.6%	$957,429	28.6%	$391,348
1999	1A	21.0%	$1,158,489	21.0%	$473,531
2000	1C	0.1%	$1,159,647	−9.1%	$430,440
2001	3B	−6.3%	$1,086,590	−11.9%	$379,217

Year	Type of Year	WSTL Return	End-of-Year Accumulation from One-Time Investment of $10,000 Using the WSTL	S&P 500 Return	End-of-Year Accumulation from One-Time Investment of $10,000 in the S&P 500
2002	3C	−12.6%	$949,679	−22.1%	$295,410
2003	3C	10.3%	$1,047,496	28.7%	$380,193
2004	3A	10.9%	$1,161,673	10.9%	$421,634
2005	1C	−0.2%	$1,159,350	4.9%	$442,294
2006	Tier 2	15.8%	$1,342,527	15.8%	$512,177
CAGR*		14.16%		11.22%	

*Compound annual growth rate

Compound Annual Growth Rate

Although the compound annual growth rate is the best measure of an investment strategy's return, many less experienced investors are not familiar with the term. Let's start with the technical definition. The **compound annual growth rate** (**CAGR**) is the average annual rate of return that, when compounded over time, accounts for the change in the total value of an investment from the beginning of a period to the end of the period, assuming that there were no withdrawals and no additional investments. Mathematically, the CAGR is *the geometric mean, not the arithmetic mean.*

That said, consider an illustration that explains why CAGR is the better measure of an investment strategy's return. Suppose you invested $10,000 at the end of 2004. For 2005 and 2006, you had returns of −20% and 20%, respectively. Accordingly, the value of your investment fell to $8,000 at the end of 2005; then rose to $9,600 at the end of 2006. The *average annual return (the arithmetic mean)* is 0%: (−20% + 20%) ÷ 2 = 0%. While accurate mathematically, the 0% obviously does not indicate the economic reality of the situation: you invested $10,000, and two years later its value was $9,600. The *CAGR (the geometric mean)* in this example is −2.02%, which correctly measures the economic reality of the situation:

Original investment	$10,000
$10,000 × −2.02% =	− 202
December 31, 2005	$ 9,798
$ 9,798 × −2.02% =	− 198
December 31, 2006	$ 9,600

The CAGRs for you and your neighbor's investment strategies are the shaded percentages on the bottom row in Exhibit 3-3. For 1970-2006, your CAGR (under the WSTL strategy) was 14.16%, and her CAGR (under buy-and-hold) was 11.22%. That means the

WSTL strategy had an impressive advantage of 2.94 percentage points. And you will see in the next chapter that the WSTL strategy's advantage is even more impressive because buying-and-holding the S&P 500 was riskier.

Recall from Chapter 1 that an investment strategy's *alpha* is the difference (measured in percentage points) between its CAGR—adjusted for risk and net of the owner's investment costs—and the CAGR of buying-and-holding a benchmark index such as the S&P 500. The WSTL's alpha for 1970-2006 was greater than 2.82 percentage points (explained on p. 10). Every professional money manager would be thrilled to achieve an alpha of even 1.0 percentage point over a 20-year period. *Had the WSTL's alpha for 1970-2006 been achieved in real-time, the strategy would be famous.*

Chapter 4

◇◇◇◇◇◇◇◇◇◇◇◇◇◇

RISK FOR 1970-2006

Power Points

1. Of the eight measures of risk calculated in this chapter for 1970-2006, all of them indicate that the WSTL strategy had lower risk than buying-and-holding the S&P 500.

2. The standard deviation of annual returns, a popular measure of risk, indicates that the WSTL had 15.5% lower risk.

3. The depth and duration of downside volatility, a more comprehensive measure of risk than the standard deviation, indicates that the WSTL had 29.7% lower risk.

4. The maximum number of years needed to avoid a loss indicates that the WSTL had 42.9% lower risk.

5. Four measures involving negative annual returns indicate that the WSTL had 37.5% to 81.6% lower risk.

6. The maximum year-to-date declines of 10% or more indicate that the WSTL had 33.8% lower risk.

An important aspect of any successful long-term investment strategy is managing and controlling risk. Risk—the uncertainty regarding the future value of an investment—is an inevitable aspect of investing, but many investors unwisely focus too much on return and not enough on risk. A main focus of the WSTL strategy is being prudent in your exposure to risk.

This chapter calculates eight measures of risk under the WSTL strategy and buy-and-hold for 1970-2006. Each measure indicates that the WSTL strategy had lower risk.

1. Variability of Annual Returns

This measure of risk is referred to as the **standard deviation**. The standard deviation is easy to understand as follows: The less an investment strategy's returns vary from year to year in relation to its mean annual return for the period studied, the smaller the standard deviation and the lower the risk. (If each year's return were the same, the standard deviation would be 0%.) For 1970-2006, the WSTL strategy had a standard deviation of 14.2% compared to 16.8% for buy-and-hold. Since the WSTL's standard deviation was 2.6 percentage points less, that represents 15.5% lower risk: $-2.6 \div 16.8 = -15.5\%$.

Although the standard deviation is a popular measure of risk and can be calculated in seconds using a computer, generally it leaves a lot to be desired. For example, suppose you invested in the S&P 500 and the current year's return was, say, 20% above the mean return for the past 20 years (including the current year). In that situation, you would be pleased with the current year's return but, being above the 20-year mean, that stellar return caused the standard deviation to *increase*. This shortcoming of the standard deviation is overcome by measuring the depth and duration of downside volatility.

2. Depth and Duration of Downside Volatility

This measure of risk—the so-called **ulcer index**—is not widely used, probably because calculating it is very time consuming. However, when the ulcer index is calculated on a daily basis (as is done in this book), it is a more comprehensive way to gauge an investment strategy's risk than the standard deviation. The ulcer index takes into account the "ulcer causing potential" of the depth and duration of declines in an investment strategy's value from its beginning value until each subsequent new high (if any) occurred through the period studied. The less the depth of declines in a strategy's market value and the shorter they are, the smaller the ulcer index and the lower the risk.

For 1970-2006, the ulcer index for the WSTL strategy was 11.6% and for buy-and-hold was 16.5%. Since the WSTL's ulcer index was 4.9 percentage points less, that represents 29.7% lower risk: $-4.9 \div 16.5 = -29.7\%$. The detailed calculations that yielded these ulcer indexes are available at thewallstreettrafficlight.com.[10]

3. Maximum Number of Years Needed to Avoid a Loss

This measure of risk is simple. To determine it, look at the "End-of-Year Accumulation" columns in Exhibit 3-3 (pp. 28-29). For the WSTL, the maximum number of years needed to avoid a loss was four—which was the 2001-2004 period. The total accumulation at the end of 2000 was $1,159,647, an amount that was not exceeded until the end of 2004. For buy-and-hold, the maximum number of years needed to avoid a loss was seven—which was the 2000-2006 period. The total accumulation at the end of 1999 was $473,531, an amount that was not exceeded until the end of 2006. Since the WSTL's maximum period was three years shorter, that represents 42.9% lower risk: $-3 \div 7 = -42.9\%$.

4. Negative Annual Returns

How would you feel if the value of your 401(k)/IRA fell by, say, 10% in a one-year period? Oh sure, I know it would be painful. But quantifying it, how would your pain compare to the pleasure you got in another one-year period when your retirement nest egg increased by 10%? High-caliber research in the field of behavioral finance found that the pain investors experience from financial losses is more than twice as intense as the pleasure they get from equal-sized gains.[11] In other words, investors tend to be very "loss averse." For that reason, the measures of risk discussed in sections 3 4 and 5 of this chapter are of utmost importance.

The simplest way to use negative annual returns to gauge risk for 1970-2006 is to compare the WSTL's worst year (it was 1974, which had a return of −16.0%) to the S&P 500's worst year (it also was 1974, which had a return of −26.5%). Although the WSTL's return for 1974 was negative, it was 10.5 percentage points better than the S&P 500's return for that year, representing 39.6% lower risk: 10.5 ÷ −26.5 = −39.6%.

The following table (derived from Exhibit 3-3) provides three more ways to measure risk using the negative annual returns during 1970-2006:

Negative Annual Returns	WSTL	S&P 500	WSTL Advantage	Extent of WSTL's Lower Risk
◆ Number of years	5	8	3 years	−3 ÷ 8 = −37.5%
◆ Mean annual return for the 5 years when the WSTL had negative returns	−7.6%	−14.1%	6.5 percentage points	6.5 ÷ −14.1 = −46.1%
◆ Mean annual return for the 8 years when the S&P 500 had negative returns	−2.3%	−12.5%	10.2 percentage points	10.2 ÷ −12.5 = −81.6%

All three measures indicate that the WSTL strategy had lower risk.

Exhibit 4-1 provides the supporting details for the last item in the table. *In each of the eight years when the S&P 500 had a negative return, there was a profitable trade.*

Exhibit 4-1

WSTL Returns for Years When the S&P 500 Returns Were Negative, 1970-2006

Year	Type of Year	WSTL Return	S&P 500 Return	Outcome of Trade
1973	1C	−3.0%	−14.7%	11.7%
1974	3C	−16.0%	−26.5%	10.5%
1977	1C	4.5%	−7.2%	11.7%
1981	1C	13.1%	−4.9%	18.0%
1990	1C	2.1%	−3.2%	5.2%*
2000	1C	0.1%	−9.1%	9.2%
2001	3B	−6.3%	−11.9%	5.6%
2002	3C	−12.6%	−22.1%	9.5%
Mean		−2.3%	−12.5%	10.2%

*This difference does not add across due to rounding.

5. Maximum Year-to-Date Declines of 10% or More

For 1970-2006, 11 of the 37 years had a maximum year-to-date decline of 10% or more in the S&P 500; that is 29.7% of the years. Exhibit 4-2 lists those declines and the accompanying maximum year-to-date declines under the WSTL strategy. The mean of the columns' declines were 21.0% and 13.9%, respectively. Since the WSTL strategy's mean maximum year-to-date decline was 7.1 percentage points less, that represents 33.8% lower risk: −7.1 ÷ 21.0 = −33.8%. That lower risk was due to the fact that *there was a profitable trade in each of the 11 years in the exhibit.*

Exhibit 4-2

WSTL Maximum Year-to-Date Declines During Years When the S&P 500 Maximum Year-to-Date Declines Were 10% or More, 1970-2006

Year	S&P 500 Maximum Year-to-Date Decline	Type of Year	WSTL Maximum Year-to-Date Decline	Outcome of Trade
1970	24.7%	3C	15.2%	13.7%
1973	21.9%	1C	12.1%	11.7%
1974	36.2%	3C	27.6%	10.5%
1977	15.6%	1C	5.1%	11.7%
1981	16.9%	1C	6.5%	18.0%
1982	16.4%	1C	6.1%	18.4%
1984	10.4%	1C	4.1%	2.4%
1990	16.4%	1C	16.4%	5.2%
2000	13.9%	1C	13.1%	9.2%
2001	26.8%	3B	22.2%	5.6%
2002	32.3%	3C	24.0%	9.5%
Mean	21.0%		13.9%	10.5%

Summary of Chapters 3 and 4

Exhibit 5-1 (p. 41) summarizes the return statistics discussed in the last chapter and the eight measures of risk discussed in this chapter. The message of the exhibit is clear: The WSTL strategy had higher returns with lower risk than buy-and-hold for 1970-2006.

PART TWO

USING THE WALL STREET TRAFFIC LIGHT STRATEGY

Chapter 5

◇◇◇◇◇◇◇◇◇◇◇◇◇

MARKET ANOMALIES

Power Points

1. A market anomaly is any investment strategy that, on a risk-adjusted basis, has generated returns greater than the market's return over a long period.

2. Many leading scholars believe that market anomalies are likely to be eliminated soon after they are divulged to the public.

3. A market anomaly, which is part of the four-year U.S. presidential cycle, has continued for many years since it became publicly known.

4. The WSTL market anomaly is being divulged to the public in this book. For investors considering whether to use the WSTL, the key question is: Will this anomaly continue?

The last two chapters presented the details for 1970-2006 of the WSTL's higher returns with lower risk compared to buying-and-holding the S&P 500. This chapter indicates that for 1935-1969 the WSTL had even better performance compared to buy-and-hold. As a result, the WSTL is a market anomaly that spans 1935-2006 (72 years).

A **market anomaly** is any investment strategy that has generated abnormal returns—returns which, after being adjusted for risk, exceeded the market's mean return over a long period. Many leading scholars believe that the abnormal returns of any market anomaly discovered and divulged to the public—for example, by publishing a book or an article describing it—will likely be eliminated as a result of the competition among investors trying to capitalize on the anomaly.[12] The WSTL anomaly became publicly known when this book was published in December 2007.

The first section of this chapter discusses a market anomaly that has continued many years since becoming publicly known. This anomaly is part of the four-year U.S.

presidential cycle. That discussion is followed by summaries of the WSTL anomaly for 1970-2006 and 1935-1969; then, two fascinating sets of facts about the anomaly provide additional insight into its lower risk.

U.S. Presidential Cycle Anomaly

The four years in this cycle are as follows:

- Year 1 is the post-election year.
- Year 2 is the midterm election year.
- Year 3 is the pre-election year.
- Year 4 is the election year.

This anomaly, which began in 1962, outperforms the S&P 500 by investing in 3-month T-bills for the January-through-September period of years 1 and 2. That is a total of 18 months (37.5%) of the four-year cycle. Since the S&P 500 has had a negative return for that time, those 18 months can be called the **unfavorable part of the presidential cycle**. The **favorable part of the presidential cycle** for investing in the S&P 500 is October through December of years 1 and 2 plus all of years 3 and 4, a total of 30 months (62.5%) of the four-year cycle.

Panel 1 of Appendix A calculates each part's total accumulation and CAGR for 1962-2006 from a one-time investment of $10,000 in the S&P 500 (including reinvested dividends). The results are as follows:

Based on S&P 500 Return	Favorable Part	Unfavorable Part
Total accumulation for 1962-2006	$1,570,637	$5,564
CAGR for 1962-2006	19.99%	−3.34%

Simply investing in 3-month T-bills during the unfavorable part of the cycle would have avoided the S&P 500's CAGR of −3.34%. Panel 2 of Appendix A indicates that the CAGR from investing in 3-month T-bills during the unfavorable part of the cycle for 1962-2006 was 6.04%. That is a 9.38 percentage points of improvement in return for the unfavorable part: 6.04% − (−3.34%) = 9.38%. Of course, there is no guarantee that this anomaly will continue in the future.

WSTL Anomaly

The WSTL is an anomaly because it achieved higher returns with lower risk than the S&P 500 for 1935-2006. This section summarizes that performance for both 1970-2006 and 1935-1969. Also, two additional aspects of the anomaly are described.

Higher Returns with Lower Risk. Exhibit 5-1 summarizes the powerful performance of the WSTL anomaly for 1970-2006.

Exhibit 5-1

Performance Summary for 1970-2006

Performance Measure	WSTL (13 round-trip trades)	Buy-and-Hold S&P 500	WSTL Advantage	WSTL Percentage Advantage
Returns				
Total accumulation from a one-time investment of $10,000 at the end of 1969 (re-investing dividends and interest, ignoring investment costs and income taxes)	$1,342,527	$512,177	$830,350	162%
Compound annual growth rate (CAGR)	14.16%	11.22%	2.94 % points	26.2%
Risk				
Variability of annual returns (standard deviation)	14.2%	16.8%	2.6 % points	15.5%
Depth and duration of downside volatility (ulcer index)	11.6%	16.5%	4.9 % points	29.7%
Maximum number of years needed to avoid a loss	4 years	7 years	3 years	42.9%
Worst year (It was 1974 under both strategies.)	−16.0%	−26.5%	10.5 % points	39.6%
Negative annual returns				
◆ Number of times	5 years	8 years	3 years	37.5%
◆ Mean annual return for WSTL's five years having negative returns	−7.6%	−14.1%	6.5 % points	46.1%
◆ Mean annual return for S&P 500's eight years having negative returns	−2.3%	−12.5%	10.2 % points	81.6%
Maximum year-to-date declines of 10% or more (mean for the 11 cases)	13.9%	21.0%	7.1 % points	33.8%

The WSTL model was developed for the 1935-1969 period using 20/20 hindsight. The model was then **back-tested** for that period. Exhibit 5-2 summarizes that performance, which will be discussed in Chapter 9 and Appendix E. The first two performance measures in the exhibit indicate that the WSTL had higher returns than buy-and-hold. Each of the other performance measures indicates that the WSTL had lower risk than buy-and-hold.

Exhibit 5-2

Performance Summary for 1935-1969

Performance Measure	WSTL (18 round-trip trades)	Buy-and-Hold S&P 500	WSTL Advantage	WSTL Percentage Advantage
Returns				
Total accumulation from a one-time investment of $10,000 at the end of 1934 (re-investing dividends and interest, ignoring investment costs and income taxes)	$1,776,418	$502,679	$1,273,739	253%
Compound annual growth rate (CAGR)	15.95%	11.84%	4.11 % points	34.7%
Risk				
Variability of annual returns (standard deviation)	18.7%	19.7%	1.0 % points	5.1%
Depth and duration of downside volatility (ulcer index)	11.2%	22.9%	11.7 % points	51.1%
Maximum number of years needed to avoid a loss	3 years	7 years	4 years	57.1%
Worst year (It was 1937 under both strategies.)	−32.0%	−35.0%	3.0 % points	8.6%
Negative annual returns				
◆ Number of times	3 years	10 years	7 years	70.0%
◆ Mean annual return for WSTL's five years having negative returns	−13.8%	−18.9%	5.1 % points	27.0%
◆ Mean annual return for S&P 500's eight years having negative returns	−0.6%	−10.4%	9.8 % points	94.2%
Maximum year-to-date declines of 10% or more (mean for the 16 cases)	11.0%	19.2%	8.2 % points	42.7%

The last chapter indicated that investors tend to be very loss averse. In that regard, two items provide additional insight into the WSTL anomaly's lower risk for 1935-2006.

1. A profitable trade occurred in every year when the S&P 500 had a negative return.

The S&P 500 return was negative for 18 of the 72 years during 1935-2006, or 25% of the time. Exhibit 5-3 indicates that in each of those years, the WSTL return was higher than the S&P 500 return—that is, *there was a profitable trade in each of the 18 years!* Moreover, the WSTL return was positive for 11 of the 18 years. That performance would have delighted risk-averse investors.

Exhibit 5-3

WSTL Returns for Years When the S&P 500 Returns Were Negative, 1935-2006

The dividing line separates the sample period from the test period.

Year	Type of Year	WSTL Return	S&P 500 Return	Outcome of Trade
1937	1B	−32.0%	−35.0%	3.0%
1939	3C	13.1%	−0.4%	13.5%
1940	1C	3.1%	−9.8%	12.9%
1941	3C	−8.0%	−11.6%	3.6%
1946	1B	1.3%	−8.1%	9.4%
1953	1C	8.5%	−1.0%	9.5%
1957	1C	1.2%	−10.8%	11.9%*
1962	1C	2.3%	−8.7%	11.0%*
1966	1B	−1.3%	−10.1%	8.8%
1969	1C	5.8%	−8.5%	14.3%
1973	1C	−3.0%	−14.7%	11.7%
1974	3C	−16.0%	−26.5%	10.5%
1977	1C	4.5%	−7.2%	11.7%
1981	1C	13.1%	−4.9%	18.0%
1990	1C	2.1%	−3.2%	5.2%*
2000	1C	0.1%	−9.1%	9.2%
2001	3B	−6.3%	−11.9%	5.6%
2002	3C	−12.6%	−22.1%	9.5%
Mean		−1.3%	−11.3%	10.0%

*This difference does not add across due to rounding.

2. **A high concentration of declines of 10% or more in the S&P 500 were in the years with trades.**

Appendix B lists all of the S&P 500's declines of 10% or more during 1935-2006. In total, there were 77 of those declines, split virtually 50-50 between the sample period and the test period. For 1935-2006, 77.9% of the declines were in years with trades (that is, 1B, 1C, 3B and 3C years). In comparison, the years with trades accounted for 53% of all the years during 1935-2006.

By raising the bar for the S&P 500's declines from 10% to 14.2%, the results are stunning: *There were 31 declines of 14.2% or more and 29 of them (93.5%) were in years with trades!* The other two declines were as follows:

1A year	From 10/05/87 to 10/19/87	−31.5%
1A year	From 07/17/98 to 08/31/98	−19.3%

The 1987 decline included the 20.5% crash on October 19th. The 1998 decline occurred at the time of the Russian debt default and contributed to the near-collapse of Long Term Capital Management, which had been a large and prestigious hedge fund. Both the 10% bar and the 14.2% bar help emphasize the low-risk aspect of the WSTL anomaly.

An Astute Observation. Without a doubt, the S&P 500 had considerable downside volatility in 1B, 1C, 3B and 3C years during 1935-2006. Without knowing about the WSTL anomaly itself, a mutual fund executive made this observation: "While every period of market volatility occurs in a different way and typically for different reasons, there is often a feeling of déjà vu associated with market fluctuations."[13] The WSTL anomaly certainly validates the executive's observation.

The Future of the WSTL Anomaly

Will the WSTL anomaly continue to achieve higher returns with lower risk than buying-and-holding the S&P 500 for, say, the 10-year period that began with 2007? Of course, the correct answer is, "time will tell." Personally, I am reluctant to bet against the WSTL anomaly. *I believe the anomaly could even represent a paradigm shift in the way many investors look at or evaluate the role that infrequent and prudent market timing can play in the management of their 401(k)s and IRAs.*

Chapter 6

◇◇◇◇◇◇◇◇◇◇◇◇◇◇◇

USER'S GUIDE TO GETTING STARTED

Power Points

1. There are three steps involved in using the WSTL model each year.

2. For a year with a trade, the sell signal is established on a particular day between the end of January and the end of April, when the conditions for a category "B" or "C" year are met. Then, on a particular day later in the year, the buy signal is triggered by whichever of three limits for the S&P 500 is reached first—the lower limit, the upper limit or the time limit.

3. The companion website for this book includes extensive material to assist investors in using the WSTL strategy.

4. This chapter recommends four low-cost S&P 500 index funds for use with the WSTL strategy. Two are no-load mutual funds suitable for 401(k)s and IRAs. The other two are exchange-traded funds (ETFs) suitable for an IRA brokerage account or a 401(k) with a brokerage option.

5. Along with using a low-cost S&P 500 index fund, the other basic aspects of implementing the WSTL strategy are using a money market fund, acting on the buy and sell signals in a timely manner, dollar-cost averaging and asset allocation considerations.

Many individual investors prefer to do most or all of the work of investing themselves, whereas others rely heavily on financial advisers. For each investor, that choice depends on three main factors: (1) knowledge of investing (defined broadly to include self-confidence, discipline and patience), (2) time available for investing and (3) the inclination to actually do the work involved in investing. In short, the factors are *knowledge, time* and *inclination.*

The first two parts of this book (Chapters 1-7) provide a necessary and sufficient body of knowledge to enable you to use the WSTL strategy. From Chapters 1-5, you learned two important facts. First, a scientific test indicated that, for 1970-2006, the WSTL achieved higher returns with lower risk than buying-and-holding the S&P 500. That superior performance was accomplished by making an average of one (round-trip) trade out of and back into a low-cost S&P 500 index fund about every three years. Second, the WSTL has been a market anomaly for 72 years (1935-2006).

In regard to having enough time available for investing, my estimate is that the WSTL strategy requires less than 10 hours a year, which includes reading a brief commentary once a month at thewallstreettrafficlight.com. By only monitoring when the color of the WSTL changes would reduce the time requirement to less than five hours a year.

After finishing this chapter and the next, you will have the basic knowledge to use the WSTL strategy to help manage your 401(k)/IRA. You are aware that using the strategy requires a small amount of time. If you decide to use the WSTL strategy, do you have the inclination to do-it-yourself? If not, hire a financial adviser to help you.

This chapter explains the three steps to follow in using the WSTL model, describes the material available at thewallstreettrafficlight.com and discusses basic aspects of implementing the WSTL strategy. Chapter 7 provides important history lessons from 1935-2006 to help strengthen your discipline and patience in using the WSTL strategy.

Yearly Use of the WSTL Model

The model involves three steps each year. The steps are related to the seven types of years: 1A, 1B, 1C, Tier 2, 3A, 3B and 3C. If desired, you can perform the steps yourself by following the instructions in this section. Otherwise, go to thewallstreettrafficlight.com and either monitor when the WSTL's color changes or see the steps performed for you each year. A complete description of the website is in the next section.

Step 1: In late December, classify the upcoming year into Tier 1, Tier 2 or Tier 3. (The WSTL is always green when the calendar year begins.) Use the following table to perform this step:

Tier	S&P 500's Two-Year Mean Annual Return Immediately Preceding the Year Being Classified
1	Above 13.6%
2	6.2% to 13.6%
3	Below 6.2%

Step 2a: If the upcoming year is in Tier 2, the WSTL stays green throughout the year. Therefore, hold a recommended S&P 500 index fund during that time.

Step 2b: If the upcoming year is in Tier 1 or Tier 3, classify it into category A, B or C. Exhibit 6-1 specifies the conditions used to perform step 2b. (Those conditions were presented in a flowchart in Chapter 2, p. 18.)

Considering all the conditions listed in Exhibit 6-1 on a time line, the classification of a 1C or 3C year can be established as early as the end of January. The classification of a 1B or 3B year is established on a particular day during the February-through- April period. And the classification of a 1A or 3A year is not established until the end of April.

Step 3a: In the case of a 1A or 3A year, the WSTL stays green throughout the year. Therefore, hold a recommended S&P 500 index fund during that time.

Step 3b: When the sell signal occurs in a 1B, 1C, 3B or 3C year (that is, the WSTL turns from green to red), sell the S&P 500 index fund and move the proceeds into a money market fund. When the buy signal occurs later in the year, the WSTL turns from red to green and stays green for the remainder of the year. At the time of this buy signal, move the amount accumulated in the money market fund back into the S&P 500 index fund.

Exhibit 6-1

Classifying 1A, 1B, 1C, 3A, 3B and 3C Years

1A or 3A year. This classification occurs when the S&P 500 meets *either of the following conditions:*

1. The lowest daily closing price during the prior year's December (the December low) is "not broken" during the January-through-April period of the year being classified, meaning that none of the S&P 500's daily closing prices during the January-through-April period were lower than the December low. (Under this condition it does not matter whether January's price change is positive or negative.)

   or

2. The prior year's December low is "broken" during January (but was not broken during the February-through-April period) of the year being classified, *and* January's price change is positive.

This classification is established *at the end of April*. The WSTL stays green throughout the year.

1B or 3B year. This classification occurs when the S&P 500 meets *both of the following conditions:*

1. The prior year's December low is broken during the February-through-April period of the year being classified. (It does not matter whether the December low is broken during January.)

   and

2. January's price change is positive.

This classification is established *on a particular day during the February-through-April period*. That day is the sell signal, the day when the WSTL turns from green to red.

1C or 3C year. This classification occurs when the S&P 500 meets *both of the following conditions:*

1. The prior year's December low is broken during the January-through-April period of the year being classified.

   and

2. January's price change is negative.

This classification is established *on a particular day between the end of January and the end of April*. That day is the sell signal, the day when the WSTL turns from green to red.

The trade in a 1B, 1C, 3B or 3C year (step 3b) is completed by determining the date of the buy signal. The buy signal is triggered by whichever of three limits the S&P 500 reaches first following the sell signal—the *lower limit*, the *upper limit* or the *time limit*. Exhibit 6-2 indicates those precise limits; their development will be explained in Appendix C, which goes with Chapter 9.

Exhibit 6-2

The Limits for Buy Signals

Type of Limit	Specification of the Limit
	1B or 3B Year
Lower	• The S&P 500 closes, for the first time after the sell signal, at least 10.38% below the prior year's closing price.
Upper	• The S&P 500 closes, for the first time after the sell signal, at least 13.85% above its closing price on the day of the sell signal.
Time	• The end of September.
	1C or 3C Year
Lower	• The S&P 500 closes, for the first time after the sell signal, at least 10.93% below its closing price on the day of the sell signal.
Upper	• The S&P 500 closes, for the first time after the sell signal, at least 16.14% above its closing price on the day of the sell signal.
Time	• The end of November.

Exhibit 6-3 expresses the model's three steps in a flowchart. Whether or not you perform the steps yourself, this exhibit serves as a handy reference.

Exhibit 6-3

Outline of the Yearly Use of the WSTL Model

- The question in the diamond is answered in late December before the upcoming year begins.

- When the answer to that question is "no" (that is, the upcoming year is classified in Tier 1 or Tier 3), the S&P 500's closing price is monitored daily (in relation to its lowest closing price in December of the prior year) from the beginning of January until the day the classification of the year in the "A" category is established at the end of April, or until the day the classification of the year in the "B" or "C" category is established by the end of April.

- For a 1B, 1C, 3B or 3C year, the S&P 500's closing price is monitored daily from the day of the sell signal until the day of the buy signal.

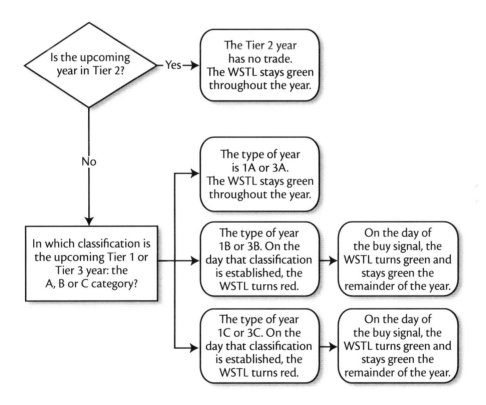

thewallstreettrafficlight.com

The companion website for this book has three purposes:

1. To save you the time that would be required to determine the buy and sell signals yourself.

2. To keep you updated on the performance of the WSTL compared to buying-and-holding the S&P 500.

3. To provide you educational material that complements the contents of this book.

The following contents of the website can be accessed without registration:

- The classification of the upcoming year into Tier 1, Tier 2 or Tier 3 in late December before the upcoming year begins.

- The line chart for December of the prior year through April of the current year, if the current year is in Tier 1 or Tier 3. The chart will be updated every weekend (or more often when a sell signal is close to occurring or does actually occur), until category A, B or C is established on or before the end of April.

- Quarterly updates that track the ongoing, real-time performance of the WSTL compared to buying-and-holding the S&P 500. The first year tracked was 2007, the year in which this book was published; 2007 is a Tier 2 year.

- The line chart for each year starting with 2007 and going back to 1935, along with a brief explanation for its classification. (Chapter 8 illustrates three line charts.)

The following contents of the website can be accessed after registering there:

- Brief monthly commentaries available at the start of the first trading day after the 14th of each month (or more often when a buy or sell signal occurs or is close to occurring). The commentaries anticipate the likely occurrence of buy and sell signals, report on those signals when they actually occur and keep you abreast of the S&P 500's short-term movements and annual returns. Typically, the commentaries are no more than a few paragraphs in length and include page references to this book. All the commentaries are archived by date.

- Tutorials, articles and other relevant information presented for educational purposes.

- The current exchange policies of the two recommended index mutual funds—Fidelity Spartan 500 Index Fund and Vanguard 500 Index Fund. Those policies, which govern the purchase and sale of the funds, are discussed in the next section.

Basics of Implementing the WSTL Strategy

Beyond using the material presented thus far in this chapter and having access to thewallstreettrafficlight.com, you need to know five basic aspects of implementing the WSTL strategy.

1. **Four Low-Cost S&P 500 Index Funds**. S&P 500 index funds are passively managed funds that mimic the S&P 500 Index's return—that is, the sum of the S&P 500's price change and its reinvested dividends. S&P 500 index funds are available in two forms: index mutual funds and exchange-traded funds. An **index mutual fund** is priced once a day (when the U.S. financial markets close at 4 p.m. eastern time), whereas an **exchange-traded fund** (**ETF**) trades on an exchange throughout the day like a stock. Considering the factors of cost, exchange policy and customer service, two no-load S&P 500 index funds are best suited to using the WSTL strategy in a 401(k)/IRA: the Fidelity Spartan 500 Index Fund and the Vanguard 500 Index Fund. Two ETFs are best suited to an IRA brokerage account or a 401(k) with a brokerage option: the Standard & Poor's Depository Receipts (SPDRs, pronounced "**Spiders**") and the iShares S&P 500 Index Fund.

   The following table compares the mean annual return of the four funds (net of all investment costs and any tracking error) to the S&P 500 Index:

Fund	Ticker Symbol	How Much the Fund Underperformed the S&P 500 Index for 2001-2006 (based on mean annual returns)
Fidelity Spartan 500 Index Fund	FSMKX	0.12% per year
Vanguard 500 Index Fund	VFINX	0.12% per year
Spiders	SPY	0.10% per year
iShares S&P 500 Index Fund	IVV	0.08% per year

   All four funds did an outstanding job of mimicking the S&P 500 for 2001-2006. Underperforming the S&P 500's annual return by only 0.12% means that *the total cost to invest each multiple of $10,000 is less than 3½ cents a day!*[14]

   Be aware that almost all S&P 500 index mutual funds have much higher annual investment costs than the Fidelity Spartan 500 Index Fund and the Vanguard 500 Index Fund. The average cost of all S&P 500 index mutual funds for 2006 was nearly 0.60%, or five times the cost of the Fidelity and Vanguard funds. In 2006, some 20 S&P 500 index mutual funds had average investment costs in excess of 1.20%![15]

   When an index mutual fund is bought or sold, the transaction is governed by the mutual fund company's **exchange policy**. In particular, it is important to know whether there would be a redemption fee when selling an index fund as well as any trading restrictions. At the time this section was being written (August 2007), the Fidelity Spartan 500 Index Fund had a 0.50% redemption fee if the fund is held for less than 90 days; the Vanguard 500 Index Fund did not allow a repurchase of the fund within 60 days after selling it. For 1970-2006, a WSTL investor would have incurred Fidelity's redemption fee only once, in 2001. Vanguard's trading restriction would have occurred only once, also in 2001. To keep updated on the exchange policies of these funds that are relevant for purposes of acting on the WSTL's buy and sell signals, go to thewallstreettrafficlight.com and click on the "Exchange Policy" you want to see.

Since ETFs are bought and sold through a broker, each buy or sell transaction has a commission. Fortunately, the WSTL's small number of transactions means that brokerage commissions are a relatively insignificant cost, especially when a discount broker is used.[16]

Not all 401(k) plans offer the Fidelity Spartan 500 Index Fund, the Vanguard 500 Index Fund or any other low-cost S&P 500 fund. In those cases, a large-cap stock fund—somewhat like the S&P 500—is almost always available. Unfortunately, the investment costs of such funds generally are *much higher* than those of a low-cost S&P 500 index fund. As a result, *those large-cap stock funds rarely outperform an S&P 500 index fund over long periods.*

If your 401(k) does not offer a low-cost S&P 500 index fund, you and fellow employees can request that one be made available. As the sponsor of the plan, your employer has a fiduciary responsibility to act in the employees' best interest. That responsibility may not be met if a low-cost index fund (at least as broad as the S&P 500) is not offered.

2. **Money Market Funds**. In previous chapters, the WSTL strategy invested in 3-month T-bills when the WSTL was red. The reason: those T-bills were available throughout 1935-2006, whereas money market funds did not become available to individual investors until the late 1970s. The rate on money market funds has tended to be slightly higher than the rate on 3-month T-bills. In using the WSTL strategy today, it is preferable—more convenient and slightly more profitable—to move into and out of a money market fund instead of T-bills.

3. **Acting on Sell and Buy Signals in a Timely Manner**. As a practical matter, sometimes you will not be able to act on the sell and buy signals until *the day after they occur*. Two reasons for this delay are: (i) a signal cannot be determined for certain until the market closes on the day in question and (ii) your schedule may not allow you to monitor the S&P 500's movement and act on a signal the day it occurs. Fortunately, Exhibit 6-4 indicates that, on average, the effect of a one-day delay in acting on the sell and buy signals was *very small*. For both types of signals, the positive and negative percentages in the exhibit have the same meaning. A positive percentage indicates an improvement in the WSTL's performance by acting on the signal one day late—that is, the S&P 500 rose the day after the sell signal occurred or fell the day after the buy signal occurred. The opposite conditions resulted in a negative percentage.

Exhibit 6-4

Acting on Sell and Buy Signals One Day Late

Date of Actual Sell Signal	Effect of Waiting One Day to Sell	Date of Actual Buy Signal	Effect of Waiting One Day to Buy
End 1/35	−0.6%	03/14/35	−2.1%
04/26/37	1.7%	06/14/37	−0.9%
03/18/38	2.2%	03/25/38	1.6%
End 1/39	1.5%	04/06/39	4.5%
End 1/40	0.0%	05/14/40	−1.0%
End 1/41	0.7%	End 11/41	Not applicable*
03/06/42	−0.9%	04/17/42	−0.8%
02/25/46	0.6%	09/03/46	−3.1%
04/14/47	0.1%	05/17/47	−0.4%
End 1/48	0.1%	End 11/48	Not applicable*
02/05/49	−0.6%	06/13/49	−0.7%
02/17/53	−0.1%	09/14/53	−0.8%
End 1/56	0.5%	End 11/56	Not applicable*
End 1/57	−0.2%	10/21/57	0.4%
End 1/60	0.6%	End 11/60	Not applicable*
End 1/62	0.6%	05/23/62	0.8%
03/01/66	−1.0%	08/01/66	0.0%
End 1/69	−0.1%	07/28/69	0.8%
End 1/70	0.9%	05/14/70	−1.9%
02/01/73	−0.4%	07/03/73	0.1%
02/11/74	0.3%	07/10/74	0.1%
End 1/77	0.5%	11/02/77	−0.1%
02/02/81	1.2%	09/25/81	−2.4%
End 1/82	−2.2%	06/21/82	−1.0%
02/03/84	−1.8%	End 11/84	Not applicable*
End 1/90	−0.1%	End 11/90	Not applicable*
End 1/00	1.1%	End 11/00	Not applicable*
02/21/01	−0.2%	03/14/01	−0.6%
End 1/02	−0.7%	06/20/02	1.7%
End 1/03	0.5%	06/11/03	−0.1%
End 1/05	0.7%	End 11/05	Not applicable*
Mean	0.2%		−0.3%

*This buy signal was triggered by the time limit for a 1C or 3C year.

Suppose, for whatever reason, you fail to act on a buy or sell signal either on the day it occurred or the following day. What should you do? Act on the signal as soon as possible thereafter.

4. **Dollar-Cost Averaging**. If you invest a set amount of money at regular intervals—such as making monthly contributions to your 401(k)—that is called **dollar-cost averaging**. Millions of investors use that systematic approach. Dollar-cost averaging can easily be adapted to the WSTL strategy. When the WSTL is green, put the regular contributions into the S&P 500 index fund already in use at that time. When the WSTL is red, put those contributions into the money market fund already in use at that time. Because of the brokerage commissions on transactions involving ETFs, dollar-cost averaging is better suited to index mutual funds.

5. **Asset Allocation Considerations**. **Asset allocation** refers to deciding on and maintaining a suitable mix of different types of investments in your portfolio. Your portfolio encompasses all of your 401(k)s, IRAs and taxable accounts.

In particular, an S&P 500-type fund (that is, a large-cap fund) is generally a core holding in an investor's portfolio. As a WSTL investor, specifically what decision do you need to make with regard to your 401(k)/IRA when a sell signal occurs? You must decide how much to decrease your asset allocation to the S&P 500 and thereby increase your asset allocation to a money market fund. Since the WSTL historically has been red only about 20% of the time, the related market timing of moving out of the S&P 500 and into a money market fund is simply *a short-term departure from your target long-term asset allocation.*

As an example, suppose that Trisha, a WSTL investor has nearly all of her portfolio in a 401(k) and an IRA. Her target long-term asset allocation has 50% of her portfolio in the S&P 500. That means the 50% allocation to the S&P 500 is her "green light" allocation. When the WSTL turns red, Trisha could go to the limit and sell her entire investment in the S&P 500 and put the proceeds into a money market fund. In that case, her "red light" allocation to the S&P 500 would be 0%. (Previous chapters implicitly assumed an allocation of 0% to the S&P 500 when the WSTL was red.)

As a less extreme change when the WSTL turns red, Trisha could sell 60% of her investment in the S&P 500 (that is, 30% of her portfolio: 50% × 60% = 30%) and put the proceeds into a money market fund. In that case, her red light allocation to the S&P 500 would be 20% (50% − 30% = 20%). Having 0% and 20% in the S&P 500 are just two of the possible allocations Trisha could choose when the WSTL is red.

It is important to note that the market cycles for the S&P 500 (large-cap stocks) often occur at different times than the market cycles for small-cap stocks, or mid-cap stocks or foreign stocks. As a result, over the years *the WSTL's buy and sell signals—which are for the S&P 500—would not have worked as well for the non-S&P 500 market segments.*

Chapter 7

◇◇◇◇◇◇◇◇◇◇◇◇◇◇◇

DISCIPLINE AND PATIENCE

Power Points

1. To help you develop sufficient discipline and patience to control your emotions and stay the course in using the WSTL strategy, this chapter presents relevant history lessons from 1935-2006.

2. Most of the events causing stock-market investors great fear occurred when the WSTL was green.

3. At any point during each period in which the WSTL is red, you "take the heat" whenever the S&P 500 has posted a net gain.

4. Ten times the WSTL investor would have been faced with the emotionally challenging decision of whether to sell the S&P 500 at a loss (that is, selling at a price lower than the purchase price at the previous year's buy signal). While the four largest losses ranged from 10.3% to 33.0%, the WSTL investor outperformed the S&P 500 in nine of the 10 trades in those cases.

5. Under the WSTL strategy, an extreme but technically correct view is that all daily financial news—except the S&P 500's daily closing prices—can be regarded as nothing more than stock market entertainment.

Look back at the performance summary in Exhibit 5-1 (p. 41). It presents the return and risk statistics of the WSTL strategy versus buying-and-holding the S&P 500 for 1970-2006. As you consider that performance, keep this critical point in mind: it would have been challenging to stay the course using either the WSTL strategy or buy-and-hold, particularly during periods of stressful declines in the S&P 500. To be successful under either strategy, investors must control their emotions—as they watch the ups and downs of the S&P 500—and let their reason prevail over the long-term.[17] However, that formula for success is much easier said than done, primarily because there is a strong tendency for investors' emotions to overpower their intellect.

Investors need considerable discipline and patience to control their emotions and maintain a sound perspective when the WSTL sell signals and buy signals occur. Those sell signals often occur near the tops of S&P 500 cycles, and the buy signals tend to occur at fearful times in the stock market. As a result, you must be highly disciplined to act on those signals in the face of substantial contrary opinion. Just as important, you need to be patient and wait for the signals to occur before you act on them. To help develop sufficient discipline and patience to stay the course in using the WSTL strategy, it is helpful to have knowledge of relevant history lessons from 1935-2006 presented in this chapter. When investors lack that knowledge, behavioral research indicates that they are prone to imagine the worst.[18] To help you understand the discipline and patience that will be required to use the WSTL strategy in the years following 2006, this chapter examines specific times that would have severely tested the WSTL investor.

Events Causing Stock-Market Investors Great Fear

When stock-market investors experience events causing great fear, they have a tendency to panic and sell. Exhibit 7-1 lists 17 of those events that occurred during 1935-2006. Interestingly, the WSTL was green for 14 of the 17 events! That means WSTL investors would have held the S&P 500 during almost as many "great-fear events" as did buy-and-hold investors. Both types of investors would have needed their intellect to subdue their fear during those stressful times.

Exhibit 7-1

Events Causing Stock-Market Investors Great Fear, 1935-2006

Year	Event (Month)	Type of Year	Buy Signal	Color of WSTL When Event Occurred
1939	World War II started (September)	3C	04/06/39	Green
1940	France fell to Germany (June)	1C	05/14/40	Green
1941	Pearl Harbor bombed (December)	3C	End 11/41	Green
1950	Korean War (started June)	Tier 2		Green
1956	Suez Canal crisis (October)	1C	End 11/56	**Red**
1957	Soviet Union launched Sputnik, the first earth-orbiting satellite (October)	1C	10/21/57	**Red**
1962	Cuban missile crisis (October)	1C	05/23/62	Green
1963	President Kennedy assassinated (November)	3A		Green
1964	Gulf of Tonkin incident off the coast of North Vietnam (August)	Tier 2		Green
1973	Arab oil embargo (October)	1C	07/03/73	Green
1979	Three Mile Island nuclear accident (March)	3A		Green
1980	Bubble in silver prices burst (January)	Tier 2		Green
1987	Biggest one-day stock market crash in U.S. history (October)	1A		Green
1990	Iraq invaded Kuwait (August)	1C	End 11/90	**Red**
1997	Asian currency crisis began in Thailand (July)	1A		Green
1998	Russian debt default (August) and near-collapse of Long Term Capital Management (September)	1A		Green
2001	Terrorist attacks on New York City and Washington D.C. (September)	3B	03/14/01	Green

Taking the Heat

At any point during each period in which the WSTL is red, the WSTL investor is **taking the heat** whenever the S&P 500 has posted a net gain (that is, buy-and-hold has outperformed the WSTL at those times). Taking the heat increases in direct proportion to the size of the S&P 500's net gain. Emotionally, it can be quite challenging to take the heat.

Exhibit 7-2 indicates the *maximum heat taken* in 1B and 3B years, and the outcome of each trade. To understand this exhibit, consider the period while the WSTL was red in 1937. On the day of the sell signal (04/26/37), the S&P 500 closed at 16.16. On the day of the buy signal (06/14/37), the S&P 500 had fallen to 15.20, resulting in a profitable trade of 3.0% (which takes into account the interest earned on T-bills and S&P 500 dividends forgone). The S&P 500's highest close between those signals was 16.73, on 05/04/37. That means the maximum heat taken in 1937 was 3.53%: (16.73 − 16.16) ÷ 16.16 = 3.53%.

Exhibit 7-2

Maximum Heat in "B" Years, 1935-2006

The line separates the sample period from the test period.

Year	Sell Signal	S&P 500's High Between Sell Signal and Buy Signal	Maximum Heat Taken (at the high between the signals)	Buy Signal	Outcome of Trade
1937	04/26/37	05/04/37	3.53%	06/14/37	3.0%
1938	03/18/38	03/19/38	2.16%	03/25/38	11.5%
1942	03/06/42	03/17/42	1.59%	04/17/42	5.9%
1946	02/25/46	05/29/46	13.84%	09/03/46	9.4%
1947	04/14/47	05/05/47	5.02%	05/17/47	2.6%
1949	02/05/49	03/29/49	2.49%	06/13/49	8.3%
1966	03/01/66	04/21/66	2.62%	08/01/66	8.8%
2001	02/21/01	02/26/01	0.99%	03/12/01	5.6%

In developing the model for the WSTL strategy during 1935-1969, the upper limit for buy signals in those years was set at 13.85% (explained in Appendix C, which goes with Chapter 9). Using that upper limit enabled the trade in 1946 to be profitable. During 1970-2006, the maximum heat taken in the only B year (2001) was a mere 0.99%.

Exhibit 7-3 indicates the maximum heat taken in 1C and 3C years, and the outcome of each trade. Note that the maximum heat taken in C years tended to be much higher than in B years. Appendix C explains that the upper limit for buy signals in 1C and 3C years was set at 16.14%. During 1970-2006, the maximum heat taken in C years was 16.57% in 2003.

Exhibit 7-3

Maximum Heat in "C" Years, 1935-2006

The line separates the sample period from the test period.

Year	Sell Signal	S&P 500's High Between Sell Signal and Buy Signal	Maximum Heat Taken (at the high between the signals)	Buy Signal	Outcome of Trade
1935	End 1/35	02/18/35	2.64%	03/14/35	17.7%
1939	End 1/39	03/10/39	6.50%	04/06/39	13.5%
1940	End 1/40	04/08/40	4.48%	05/14/40	12.9%
1941	End 1/41	09/17/41	3.97%	End 11/41	3.6%
1948	End 1/48	06/15/48	16.13%	End 11/48	−4.7%
1953	02/17/53	03/17/53	3.25%	09/14/53	9.5%
1956	End 1/56	08/02/56	13.51%	End 11/56	−4.0%
1957	End 1/57	07/15/57	9.86%	10/21/57	11.9%
1960	End 1/60	08/24/60	4.42%	End 11/60	−0.5%
1962	End 1/62	03/15/62	3.22%	05/23/62	11.0%
1969	End 1/69	05/14/69	3.06%	07/28/69	14.3%
1970	End 1/70	03/03/70	6.25%	05/14/70	13.7%
1973	02/01/73	02/13/73	1.76%	07/03/73	11.7%
1974	02/11/74	03/13/74	10.02%	07/10/74	10.5%
1977	End 1/77	02/01/77	0.50%	11/02/77	11.7%
1981	02/02/81	03/25/81	8.04%	09/25/81	18.0%
1982	End 1/82	End 1/82	0.00%	06/21/82	18.4%
1984	02/03/84	05/02/84	0.62%	End 11/84	2.4%
1990	End 1/90	07/16/90	12.12%	End 11/90	5.2%
2000	End 1/00	03/24/00	9.54%	End 11/00	9.2%
2002	End 1/02	03/19/02	3.55%	06/20/02	9.5%
2003	End 1/03	06/11/03	16.57%	06/11/03	−18.4%
2005	End 1/05	11/25/05	7.36%	End 11/05	−5.1%

Selling the S&P 500 at a Loss

It is important to distinguish between an *unprofitable trade* and *selling the S&P 500 at a loss*. An unprofitable trade results from the fact that, for the period when the WSTL is red, the S&P 500 return is greater than the interest the WSTL investor earned on 3-month T-bills. Consequently, for a year in which an unprofitable trade occurs, the WSTL return is less than the S&P 500 return. History tells us that having an unprofitable trade, on average, about once every 14 years during 1935-2006 is an unpleasant but inherent aspect of the WSTL strategy.

On the other hand, selling the S&P 500 at a loss refers to a decline in the S&P 500 *from the day of the buy signal in one year to the day of the sell signal in the following year*. Such declines in the S&P 500 are not unprofitable trades because the outcome of a trade measures what occurred *from the day of a sell signal to the day of the buy signal within the same year*.

It would require considerable discipline and patience for investors to sell the S&P 500 at a loss when the WSTL turns red. But, Exhibit 7-4 indicates that decision would have been wise. The exhibit presents the 10 cases where the WSTL investor would have been faced with selling the S&P 500 at a loss. The average of those losses—the mean of the S&P 500's decline from the buy signal to the sell signal—was 9.2%. The four largest losses were 33.0%, 15.0%, 11.0% and 10.3%. The 10 buy signals following those sell signals resulted in trades that had *an average profit of 5.8%. Nine of the 10 trades were profitable.*

Exhibit 7-4

Selling the S&P 500 at a Loss, 1935-2006

Each case involved trades in back-to-back years.

Case	Buy Signal	Sell Signal	S&P 500 Decline from Buy Signal to Sell Signal	Outcome of Trade in Year of Sell Signal
1	06/14/37	03/18/38	33.0%	11.6%
2	05/14/40	End 1/41	2.0%	3.7%
3	End 11/41	03/06/42	10.3%	6.2%
4	09/03/46	04/14/47	5.7%	2.8%
5	End 11/56	End 1/57	0.8%	12.0%
6	07/28/69	End 1/70	5.8%	13.9%
7	07/03/73	02/11/74	11.0%	10.6%
8	End 11/00	02/21/01	4.5%	5.7%
9	03/12/01	End 1/02	4.2%	9.5%
10	06/20/02	End 1/03	15.0%	−18.4%
Mean			9.2%	5.8%

Stock Market Entertainment

The WSTL model is based entirely on the S&P 500's annual returns and its daily closing prices. That information determines the buy and sell signals, which are anticipated, reported and monitored at thewallstreettrafficlight.com.

Using the WSTL strategy can be entertaining, somewhat like watching a sporting event. In most cases during 1935-2006, classifying Tier 2 years was akin to knowing which team will win *before the game starts*; that's because, in Tier 2 years, the mean return was far above average and the risk was far below average. Also, in most cases, classifying 1B, 1C, 3B and 3C years by the end of April was akin to knowing which team will win *soon after the game starts*; that's because 26 of the 31 trades were profitable and only one of the unprofitable trades lost more than 5.1%.

As a WSTL investor, you are a "WSTL fan." While the WSTL is green, you root for the S&P 500 to rise. While the WSTL is red, you root for the S&P 500 to fall. Although being a WSTL fan would have been frustrating at times, your "team" has had very enviable performance during 1935-2006. As a WSTL fan, it certainly will be exciting to participate in the team's performance in the years following 2006.

Given the important role of the S&P 500's daily closing prices in the WSTL model, I refer to all daily financial news—excluding those prices—as "other financial news." As a WSTL investor, you have the option to completely ignore other financial news. As a practical matter, however, other financial news can educate and entertain you; it is often interesting and intellectually stimulating. The potential danger of other financial news is that it also may be emotionally stimulating. The examples in this chapter underscore the fact that you *should not* let your emotions interfere with acting on the WSTL signals, because history is on your side.

PART THREE

DEVELOPING AND TESTING THE WALL STREET TRAFFIC LIGHT MODEL

Chapter 8

CLASSIFYING CATEGORY A, B AND C YEARS DURING 1935-1969

Power Points

1. The WSTL model, which is based on the S&P 500's annual returns and its daily closing prices from 1935-1969 (a 35-year period), was developed in four steps.

2. Step 1, described in this chapter, classifies all 35 years into the A, B and C categories. (The next chapter describes the other three steps.)

3. This chapter illustrates how to use line charts to classify years into the A, B and C categories.

Chapters 8, 9 and 10 develop and test the WSTL model. That detailed material will be of particular interest to experienced individual investors, financial advisers, market strategists, professional money managers and members of the academic community. If you don't want to get involved in the details of those three chapters, skip to Chapter 11 now.

Using the S&P 500's daily closing prices and annual returns from 1935-1969, the WSTL model was developed for the sample period. After developing the model, it was applied to 1970-2006, the test period. Exhibit 5-1 (p. 41) summarized the model's market-beating performance for the test period.

The following steps were used to develop the WSTL model:

Step 1: Each year during 1935-1969 was classified into category A, B or C.

Step 2: The outcome of each trade (out of and back into the S&P 500) in a category B and C year was calculated.

Step 3: Each year during 1935-1969 was classified into Tier 1, Tier 2 or Tier 3.

Step 4: Of the trades under step 2, only the ones in a tier(s) whose trades considered together had a strong tendency to be profitable were retained.

This chapter performs step 1. The next chapter performs the other three steps; in particular, step 3 is based on the strong tendency of the S&P 500's annual returns to revert to their long-term mean.

It is important to note that step 3 to *develop* the WSTL model became step 1 to *use* the model. The reason the order changes will be apparent in the next chapter. (Chapter 6 presented and explained the three steps to use the model, pp. 46-47.)

This chapter illustrates how to use line charts to apply the specific conditions defining category A, B and C years. Line charts are the ultimate in simplicity because no mathematical calculations are required to prepare or interpret them. The main focus of each chart is whether the S&P 500's December low was broken during the ensuing January-through-April period.

Line Chart for a Category "A" Year

The classification of a category "A" year is established when the S&P 500 meets either of two conditions:

1. The lowest daily closing price during the prior year's December (the December low) was not broken during the January-through-April period of the year being classified. "Not broken" means that none of the S&P 500's daily closing prices during the January-through-April period were lower than the December low. (Note that under this condition it does not matter whether January's price change was positive or negative.)

    or

2. The prior year's December low was broken during January (but not during the February-through-April period) of the year being classified, *and* January's price change was positive.

The classification of a category "A" year is established at the end of April. The WSTL is green throughout category "A" years.

The conditions for a category "A" year, as well as the conditions for category "B" and "C" years, were developed by using 20/20 hindsight to analyze the S&P 500's daily closing prices for the prior year's December-through-April period of each year during 1935-1969.

There were 16 category "A" years during 1935-1969. We will look at the line chart for one of those years, 1954. As explained below, the S&P 500's movements during the five-month period of December 1953 through April 1954 played a major role in developing the WSTL model.

Exhibit 8-1 depicts the S&P 500's daily closing prices for December 1953 through April 1954. In developing the WSTL model, 1954 was classified as a category "A" year because the December low was not broken during the ensuing January-through-April period. That is, condition 1 was met.

Exhibit 8-1

S&P 500 Daily Closing Prices for December 1953 through April 1954

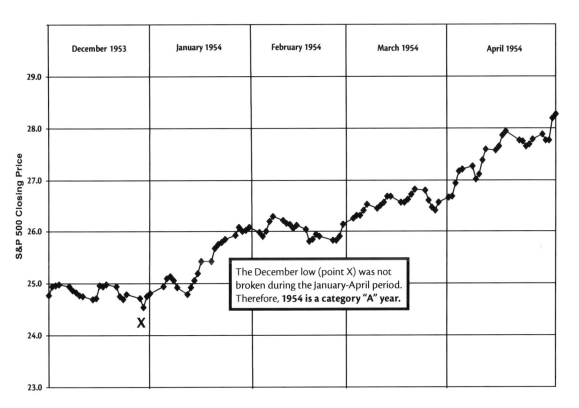

The classification of 1954 as a category "A" year was important in developing the WSTL model. That's because, of all the category "A" years during 1935-1969, the S&P 500 came the closest in January 1954 to breaking the prior year's December low. Specifically, the January 1954 low (24.80 on the 11th) was only 1.05% higher than the December 1953 low (24.55 on the 29th). That near miss was helpful in developing the model because the S&P 500 return for 1954 was 52.6%, the highest of any year during 1935-1969. Consequently, even though the December 1953 low was not broken in January 1954 along with the fact that January's price change was positive, it was prudent to include condition 2 in the model as a second way in which the classification of a category "A" year could be established.

Condition 2: The prior year's December low was broken during January (but not during the February-through-April period) of the year being classified, and January's price change was positive.

Condition 2 represents a potentially valuable "safety net" that protects against the possibility of the December low being broken during January (especially when the December low occurred late in the month) in what otherwise would have been a category "A" year under condition 1.

Exhibit 8-2 presents the details of classifying all of the category "A" years during 1935-1969. Those classifications were established at the end of April. All of the classifications were based on condition 1.

Exhibit 8-2

Establishing the Classifications of the Category "A" Years, 1935-1969

Year	Prior Year's December Low		Was December Low Broken in the January-through-April Period?
	Date	S&P 500	
1936	12/16/35	12.73	No
1943	12/01/42	9.28	No
1944	12/01/43	11.13	No
1945	12/01/44	12.80	No
1950	12/01/49	16.15	No
1951	12/04/50	19.00	No
1952	12/01/51	22.94	No
1954	12/29/53	24.55	No
1955	12/01/54	33.99	No
1958	12/18/57	39.38	No
1959	12/02/58	52.46	No
1961	12/01/60	55.30	No
1963	12/03/62	61.94	No
1964	12/03/63	73.62	No
1965	12/15/64	83.22	No
1967	12/01/66	80.08	No

Line Chart for a Category "B" Year

The classification of a category "B" year is established when the S&P 500 meets *both of the following conditions:*

1. The prior year's December low was broken during the February-through-April period of the year being classified. (It does not matter whether the December low was broken during January.)

   and

2. January's price change was positive.

The classification of a category "B" year is established on a particular day during the February-through-April period. That day is the sell signal, the day when the WSTL turns from green to red.

The last category "B" year during 1935-1969 was 1966. Exhibit 8-3 depicts the S&P

500's daily closing prices for December 1965 through April 1966. 1966 was classified as a category "B" year because the December low was broken on March 1st, *and* January's price change was positive (meeting the two conditions for a category "B" year). That means the sell signal occurred on 03/01/66, the date the classification was established.

Exhibit 8-3

S&P 500 Daily Closing Prices for December 1965 through April 1966

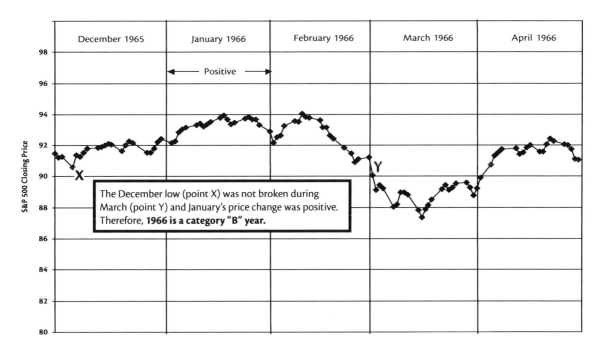

Exhibit 8-4 presents the details of classifying the category "B" years during 1935-1969. Those classifications were established (and the corresponding sell signals occurred) between February 5th and April 26th. Note that, since the S&P 500 must fall before a sell signal can occur in a category "B" year, none of those sell signals were at the exact top of a market cycle.

Exhibit 8-4

Establishing the Classifications of the Category "B" Years, 1935 - 1969

Year	Prior Year's December Low		December Low Broken in the February-through-April Period		January Change
	Date	S&P 500	Date	S&P 500	
1937	12/21/36	16.65	04/26/37	16.16	3.8%
1938	12/28/37	10.31	03/18/38	10.19	1.3%
1942	12/29/41	8.37	03/06/42	8.16	1.4%
1946	12/17/45	16.94	02/25/46	16.91	7.0%
1947	12/02/46	14.44	04/14/47	14.14	2.4%
1949	12/02/48	15.00	02/05/49	14.85	0.1%
1966	12/06/65	90.59	03/01/66	90.06	0.5%

Line Chart for a Category "C" Year

The classification of a category "C" year is established when the S&P 500 meets *both of the following conditions:*

1. The prior year's December low was broken during the January-through-April period of the year being classified.

    and

2. January's price change was negative.

The classification of a category "C" year is established on a particular day between the end of January and the end of April. That day is the sell signal, the day when the WSTL turns from green to red.

The last category "C" year during 1935-1969 was 1969. Exhibit 8-5 depicts the S&P 500's daily closing prices for December 1968 through April 1969. 1969 was classified as a category "C" year because the December low was broken in January (on the 6th), *and* January's price change was negative (meeting the two conditions for a category "C" year). That means the sell signal occurred at the end of January 1969.

Exhibit 8-5

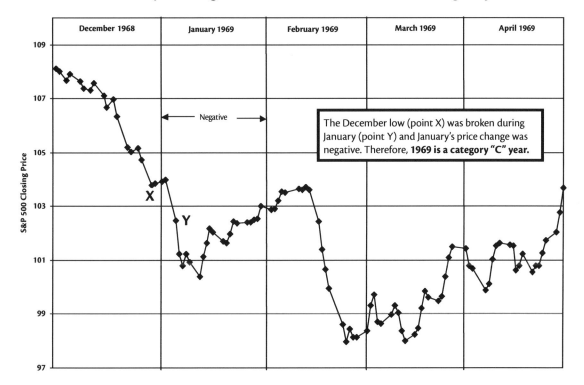

S&P 500 Daily Closing Prices for December 1968 through April 1969

The December low (point X) was broken during January (point Y) and January's price change was negative. Therefore, **1969 is a category "C" year.**

Exhibit 8-6 presents the details of classifying the category "C" years during 1935-1969. Eleven of those classifications were established at the end of January, the earliest they could occur. The classification of the other category "C" year was established on February 17th. The date that each category "C" year's classification was established is a sell signal. Since the S&P 500 must fall before a sell signal can occur in a category "C" year, none of those sell signals were at the exact top of a market cycle.

Exhibit 8-6

Establishing the Classifications of the Category "C" Years, 1935-1969

Year	Prior Year's December Low		December Low Broken in the January-through-April Period		January Change
	Date	S&P 500	Date	S&P 500	
1935	12/20/34	9.02	01/15/35	8.96	−4.2%
1939	12/09/38	12.32	01/23/39	11.93	−6.9%
1940	12/12/39	12.19	01/12/40	12.13	−3.5%
1941	12/23/40	10.38	01/21/41	10.37	−4.8%
1948	12/06/47	14.61	01/21/48	14.54	−4.0%
1953	12/04/52	25.61	02/17/53	25.50	−0.7%
1956	12/20/55	44.95	01/09/56	44.51	−3.6%
1957	12/04/56	45.84	01/15/57	45.18	−4.2%
1960	12/02/59	58.60	01/12/60	58.41	−7.1%
1962	12/21/61	70.86	01/04/62	70.64	−3.8%
1968	12/01/67	94.50	01/22/68	94.03	−4.4%
1969	12/30/68	103.80	01/06/69	102.47	−0.8%

Key Feature of the Model

Under the conditions specified to classify category A, B and C years, the WSTL is always green for the entire month of January. That means each year begins on an optimistic note regarding the S&P 500's return for January. That optimism is warranted because the S&P 500's mean return for January was 0.9% for 1935-1969. The S&P 500 rose for 23 of the 35 Januarys during that period.

Chapter 9

◇◇◇◇◇◇◇◇◇◇◇◇◇◇

COMPLETING THE MODEL

Power Points

1. Under step 2 of the four-step process used to develop the WSTL model, there were 19 trades in category B and C years during 1935-1969. Fifteen of the trades were profitable.

2. Based on the S&P 500's two-year mean annual returns and the outcomes of the trades under step 2, step 3 determined the specifications for Tier 1, Tier 2 and Tier 3.

3. Step 4 led to the conclusion that trades should not be made in Tier 2 years. As a result, the largest unprofitable trade under step 2 was eliminated, leaving 18 trades during 1935-1969.

4. The buy signal for 9 of the 18 trades was on or near the day of the S&P 500's lowest closing price of the year.

The following steps, set forth in the last chapter, were used to develop the WSTL model:

> **Step 1:** Each year during 1935-1969 was classified into category A, B or C.

> **Step 2:** The outcome of each trade (out of and back into the S&P 500) in a category B and C year was calculated.

> **Step 3:** Each year during 1935-1969 was classified into Tier 1, Tier 2 or Tier 3.

> **Step 4:** Of the trades under step 2, only the ones in a tier(s) whose trades considered together had a strong tendency to be profitable were retained.

The previous chapter explained how step 1 was performed. This chapter explains how the other steps were performed.

Step 2: Calculating the Outcomes of Trades in Category "B" and "C" Years

Note: The trades under step 2 were *prospective in nature* because each trade was subject to being eliminated under step 4.

Each trade under step 2 was conducted in the following manner. On the day of the sell signal (the day the classification of each category "B" and "C" year was established), the S&P 500 was sold and the proceeds were put into 3-month T-bills. Then on the day of the buy signal, the S&P 500 was bought with the funds accumulated in the T-bills. The WSTL was red from the sell signal to the buy signal.

Why did the WSTL strategy invest in 3-month T-bills rather than a money market fund while the WSTL was red? Those T-bills, an essentially risk-free investment, were used because of their availability throughout 1935-1969. Money market funds did not become available to individual investors until the late 1970s. The rate on 3-month T-bills tends to be slightly less than the rate on money market funds.

Keep in mind that the WSTL strategy does not receive S&P 500 dividends while the WSTL is red. This point is important because *reinvested dividends accounted for just over 38% of the S&P 500's mean annual return for 1935-1969.* The other 62% of the return was attributable to the S&P 500's price increase.

Exhibit 9-1 summarizes the 19 trades in the category "B" and "C" years during 1935-1969 under step 2. Panel 1 in the exhibit indicates that the mean return for the seven category "B" years was 7.1% higher for the WSTL model than for buying-and-holding the S&P 500. All of those trades were profitable. By definition, when a profitable trade occurred, the WSTL return for that year was greater than the S&P 500 return.

Panel 2 of Exhibit 9-1 indicates that the mean return for the 12 category "C" years was 6.0% higher for the WSTL model than for buy-and-hold. Eight of the trades were profitable and four were unprofitable. When an unprofitable trade occurred, it meant the WSTL return for that year was less than the S&P 500 return. The largest unprofitable trade (in 1968) lost 13.8%. The other unprofitable trades had losses of 4.7%, 4.0% and 0.5%.

The main driver of the profitable trades in Exhibit 9-1 is that the S&P 500 had a sizable fall for the period in which the WSTL was red. All of the unprofitable trades during 1935-1969, except the one in 1960, saw the S&P 500 rise for the period in which the WSTL was red. In the case of 1960, there was a slight *fall* in the S&P 500, but it was more than offset by the forgone dividends being greater than the interest earned from 3-month T-bills.

Exhibit 9-1

_____

The Trades Under Step 2, 1935-1969

Panel 1: Category "B" Years

Year	WSTL Return	S&P 500 Return	Outcome of Trade
1937	−32.0%	−35.0%	3.0%
1938	42.7%	31.1%	11.5%*
1942	26.2%	20.3%	5.9%
1946	1.3%	−8.1%	9.4%
1947	8.3%	5.7%	2.6%
1949	27.0%	18.8%	8.3%*
1966	−1.3%	−10.1%	8.8%
Mean	10.3%	3.2%	7.1%

Panel 2: Category "C" Years

Year	WSTL Return	S&P 500 Return	Outcome Of Trade
1935	65.4%	47.7%	17.7%
1939	13.1%	−0.4%	13.5%
1940	3.1%	−9.8%	12.9%
1941	−8.0%	−11.6%	3.6%
1948	0.9%	5.5%	−4.7%*
1953	8.5%	−1.0%	9.5%
1956	2.6%	6.6%	−4.0%
1957	1.2%	−10.8%	11.9%*
1960	0.0%	0.5%	−0.5%
1962	2.3%	−8.7%	11.0%
1968	−2.8%	11.1%	−13.8%*
1969	5.8%	−8.5%	14.3%
Mean	7.7%	1.7%	6.0%

*This difference does not add across due to rounding.

Appendices C and D

The sell signal for each category "B" and "C" year during 1935-1969 occurred on the day the classification of that year was established. The buy signal occurred later in each of those years. Appendix C explains how the precise limits that triggered the buy signals were set. Each buy signal was triggered by *whichever of three limits was reached first*: (1) the lower limit for the S&P 500's closing price, (2) the upper limit for the S&P 500's closing price or (3) the time limit. The upper limit was a "stop loss" because it confined the size of an unprofitable trade. Appendix D explains the detailed calculations necessary to determine the WSTL return for each category "B" and "C" year in Exhibit 9-1.

Step 3: Classifying Years during 1935-1969 into Tier 1, Tier 2 and Tier 3

This step is based on the strong tendency of the S&P 500 annual returns to revert to their mean return, which was 13.6% for 1935-1969. The specifications for the three tiers are as follows:

Tier	S&P 500's Two-Year Mean Annual Return Immediately Preceding the Year Being Classified
1	Above 13.6%
2	6.2% to 13.6%
3	Below 6.2%

As explained below, these specifications were determined from data in Exhibit 9-2.

The third column in Exhibit 9-2 presents the S&P 500's mean annual return for the two-year period immediately preceding each year during 1935-1969 (that is, 1933-34 preceded 1935, 1934-35 preceded 1936...and 1967-68 preceded 1969). Those returns are ranked in order from best to worst. They ranged from 42.1% for 1954-55 to −10.7% for 1940-41.

Exhibit 9-2

Analysis of S&P 500's Two-Year Mean Annual Return Preceding Each Year During 1935-1969

Row	Two-Year Period	S&P 500 Two-Year Mean Annual Return (ranked best to worst)	Year Immediately after the Two-Year Period				
			Year	Category	WSTL Return	S&P 500 Return	Outcome of Trade (under step 2)
Tier 1: Two-Year Mean Annual Return Above 13.6%							
1	1954-55	42.1%	1956	C	2.6%	6.6%	−4.0%
2	1935-36	40.8%	1937	B	−32.0%	−35.0%	3.0%
3	1944-45	28.1%	1946	B	1.3%	−8.1%	9.4%
4	1950-51	27.9%	1952	A	18.4%	18.4%	
5	1958-59	27.7%	1960	C	0.0%	0.5%	−0.5%
6	1933-34	26.3%	1935	C	65.4%	47.7%	17.7%
7	1953-54	25.8%	1955	A	31.6%	31.6%	
8	1949-50	25.3%	1951	A	24.0%	24.0%	
9	1934-35	23.1%	1936	A	33.9%	33.9%	
10	1942-43	23.1%	1944	A	19.8%	19.8%	
11	1943-44	22.8%	1945	A	36.4%	36.4%	
12	1951-52	21.2%	1953	C	8.5%	−1.0%	9.5%
13	1963-64	19.6%	1965	A	12.5%	12.5%	
14	1955-56	19.1%	1957	C	1.2%	−10.8%	11.9%*
15	1967-68	17.5%	1969	C	5.8%	−8.5%	14.3%
16	1957-58	16.3%	1959	A	12.0%	12.0%	
17	1938-39	15.4%	1940	C	3.1%	−9.8%	12.9%
18	1964-65	14.5%	1966	B	−1.3%	−10.1%	8.8%
19	1945-46	14.2%	1947	B	8.3%	5.7%	2.6%
20	1960-61	13.7%	1962	C	2.3%	−8.7%	11.0%
Mean for Tier 1					12.7%	7.9%	8.1%
Tier 2: Two-Year Mean Annual Return From 6.2% to 13.6%							
21	1948-49	12.1%	1950	A	31.7%	31.7%	
22	1961-62	9.1%	1963	A	22.8%	22.8%	
23	1952-53	8.7%	1954	A	52.6%	52.6%	
24	1962-63	7.0%	1964	A	16.5%	16.5%	
25	1966-67	7.0%	1968	C	−2.8%	11.1%	−13.8%*
26	1959-60	6.2%	1961	A	26.9%	26.9%	
Mean for Tier 2					24.6%	26.9%	−13.8%

*This difference does not add across due to rounding.

Exhibit 9-2 continues on the next page.

Exhibit 9-2 (continued)

Row	Two-Year Period	S&P 500 Two-Year Mean Annual Return (ranked best to worst)	Year Immediately after the Two-Year Period				
			Year	Category	WSTL Return	S&P 500 Return	Outcome of Trade (under step 2)
	Tier 3: Two-Year Mean Annual Return Below 6.2%
27	1947-48	5.6%	1949	B	27.0%	18.8%	8.3%*
28	1941-42	4.4%	1943	A	25.9%	25.9%	
29	1965-66	1.2%	1967	A	24.0%	24.0%	
30	1936-37	−0.6%	1938	B	42.7%	31.1%	11.5%*
31	1946-47	−1.2%	1948	C	0.9%	5.5%	−4.7%*
32	1937-38	−2.0%	1939	C	13.1%	−0.4%	13.5%
33	1956-57	−2.1%	1958	A	43.4%	43.4%	
34	1939-40	−5.1%	1941	C	−8.0%	−11.6%	3.6%
35	1940-41	−10.7%	1942	B	26.2%	20.3%	5.9%
Mean for Tier 3					21.7%	17.4%	6.4%

*This difference does not add across due to rounding.

The specifications for Tier 1 and Tier 3 were set such that they included the profitable trades in rows 20 and 27, respectively. The specification of "above 13.6%" for Tier 1 excluded row 21 from that tier. The specification of "below 6.2%" for Tier 3 excluded row 26 from that tier. The resulting specification for Tier 2 was "6.2% to 13.6%." As explained in step 4, the specification for Tier 2 eliminated the large unprofitable trade in 1968 (see row 25) but retained all the profitable trades.

Note an important point. Having established the specifications for the three tiers using the S&P 500's two-year returns immediately preceding each year during 1935-1969, each upcoming year (starting with 1970) were classified into a particular tier *before the year began*. For example, since the S&P 500's mean annual return for 1968-69 was 1.3% [(the sum of the 11.1% return for 1968 and the −8.5% return for 1969) ÷ 2 = 1.3%], 1970 was classified into Tier 3 before that year began.

Step 4: Retaining Only the Trades in a Tier(s) Whose Trades Considered Together Had a Strong Tendency to be Profitable

The following table summarizes Exhibit 9-2:

Tier	Number of Years	Number of Trades	Mean Profit per Trade
1	20	12	8.1%
2	6	1	−13.8%
3	9	6	6.4%
	35	19	

Those shaded percentages, which also are the shaded in Exhibit 9-2, indicate that the performance of the WSTL model would have been improved by eliminating the large unprofitable trade in the Tier 2 year. *As a result, the WSTL model was completed by adding the stipulation that trades will not be made in Tier 2 years.*

Look at the percentage data in the "Year Immediately after the Two-Year Period" columns in Exhibit 9-2. The reversion-to-the-mean principle provides a strong rationale for those results as follows:

1. For the years in Tier 1 (where the two-year mean annual returns immediately preceding them were above the 13.6% annual mean for 1935-1969), the S&P 500 returns tended to fall far below the mean unless they were category "A" years. The eight category "A" years had a mean return of 23.6%; those returns ranged from 12.0% to 36.4%. The twelve category "B" and "C" years in Tier 1 had a mean profit per trade of 8.1%. There were two unprofitable trades: a loss of 4.0% in 1956 and a loss of 0.5% in 1960.

2. For the Tier 2 years (where the two-year mean annual returns immediately preceding them ranged from 6.2% to 13.6%), the S&P 500 returns tended to be far above the mean. The mean return for the six Tier 2 years was 26.9%; those returns ranged from 11.1% to 52.6%.

3. For the years in Tier 3 (where the two-year mean annual returns immediately preceding them were below 6.2%), the S&P 500 returns for category "A" years were far above the annual mean of 13.6% for 1935-1969. The three category "A" years had a mean return of 31.1%. The six category "B" and "C" years in Tier 3 had a mean profit per trade of 6.4%. There was one unprofitable trade; a loss 4.7% in 1948.

Exhibit 9-3 summarizes the 18 trades for 1935-1969 under step 4. Each year in the "Type of Year" column combines the Tier 1 or Tier 3 classification and category "B" or "C."

Exhibit 9-3

The Completed Model's Eighteen Trades, 1935-1969

Year	Type of Year	Trigger for Buy Signal	WSTL Return	S&P 500 Return	Outcome of Trade
1935	1C	Lower limit	65.4%	47.7%	17.7%
1937	1B	Lower limit	−32.0%	−35.0%	3.0%
1938	3B	Lower limit	42.7%	31.1%	11.5%*
1939	3C	Lower limit	13.1%	−0.4%	13.5%
1940	1C	Lower limit	3.1%	−9.8%	12.9%
1941	3C	Time limit	−8.0%	−11.6%	3.6%
1942	3B	Lower limit	26.2%	20.3%	5.9%
1946	1B	Lower limit	1.3%	−8.1%	9.4%
1947	1B	Lower limit	8.3%	5.7%	2.6%
1948	3C	Time limit	0.9%	5.5%	−4.7%*
1949	3B	Lower limit	27.0%	18.8%	8.3%*
1953	1C	Lower limit	8.5%	−1.0%	9.5%
1956	1C	Time limit	2.6%	6.6%	−4.0%
1957	1C	Lower limit	1.2%	−10.8%	11.9%*
1960	1C	Time limit	0.0%	0.5%	−0.5%
1962	1C	Lower limit	2.3%	−8.7%	11.0%*
1966	1B	Lower limit	−1.3%	−10.1%	8.8%
1969	1C	Lower limit	5.8%	−8.5%	14.3%
Mean			9.3%	1.8%	7.5%

*This difference does not add across due to rounding.

The completed WSTL model incorporated historical patterns that repeated themselves with a high degree of consistency during 1935-1969. *As noted in Chapters 1-4, those patterns also repeated themselves with a high degree of consistency during 1970-2006.*

Appendix E

In developing the WSTL model, 20/20 hindsight was used to maximize the returns during 1935-1969. Appendix E *back-tests* the model for 1935-1969.

A Close Look at Selected Buy Signals

Following the sell signals in the 1B, 3B, 1C and 3C years, the buy signals occur later in the year, at which time the WSTL turns from red to green. Appendix C explains that if the lower limit is reached first, it always triggers the buy signal on a day when the S&P 500 fell. As a result, it is possible that the buy signal could occur on or near the day of the S&P 500's lowest closing price during the year. Exhibit 9-4 indicates that outcome did happen for *eight of the eighteen buy signals during 1935-1969*! The extraordinary timing of those eight buy signals is a key factor in the WSTL model's superiority over buy-and-hold for that period.

Exhibit 9-4

Buy Signals At or Near the S&P 500's Lowest Closing Price of the Year

Year	Type of Year	Buy Signal	Year's Low	Trading Days from Buy Signal to Year's Low
1935	1C	03/14/35	03/14/35	0
1938	3B	03/25/38	03/31/38	5
1939	3C	04/06/39	04/08/39	1
1942	3B	04/17/42	04/28/42	9
1947	1B	05/17/47	05/17/47	0
1949	3B	06/13/49	06/13/49	0
1953	1C	09/14/53	09/14/53	0
1957	1C	10/21/57	10/22/57	1

Chapter 10

◇◇◇◇◇◇◇◇◇◇◇◇◇◇◇◇◇

TESTING THE MODEL FOR 1970-2006

Power Points

1. For the test period, there were eighteen years in Tier 1, eight years in Tier 2 and eleven years in Tier 3.

2. For the test period, there were thirteen trades—eight in 1C years, one in the 3B year and four in 3C years. All of the sell signals occurred between the end of January and February 21st.

3. Eleven of the thirteen trades were profitable. The mean profit per trade was 7.1%.

4. Two of the thirteen buy signals occurred on the date of the S&P 500's low for the year.

This chapter uses a three-step approach for 1970-2006 to simulate the use of the WSTL model versus buying-and-holding the S&P 500. In other words, the WSTL model was applied to each year during 1970-2006 *as if* that year was unfolding in real-time. Since the model was developed during 1935-1969, this is a powerful and simple scientific test. Chapters 3 and 4 compared the returns and risk of those two strategies for 1970-2006.

Step 1: Classify Each Year during 1970-2006 into Tier 1, Tier 2 or Tier 3

To perform this step, it was necessary to calculate the S&P 500's mean annual return for the two-year period immediately preceding each year during 1970-2006. That is, 1968-69 preceded 1970, 1969-70 preceded 1971...and 2004-05 preceded 2006. The specifications for the three tiers developed in the previous chapter for 1935-1969 were used for 1970-2006 as follows:

Tier	S&P 500's Two-Year Mean Annual Return Immediately Preceding the Year Being Classified
1	Above 13.6%
2	6.2% to 13.6%
3	Below 6.2%

Exhibit 10-1 classifies the years during 1970-2006 into the three tiers. The two-year mean annual returns in the exhibit are ranked from best to worst, ranging from 31.0% for 1997-98 to −20.6% for 1973-74. There were eighteen years in Tier 1, eight years in Tier 2 and eleven years in Tier 3.

Exhibit 10-1

Analysis of S&P 500's Two-Year Mean Annual Returns, 1970-2006

Row	Two-Year Period	S&P 500 Two-Year Mean Annual Return (ranked best to worst)	Year Immediately after the Two-Year Period
		Tier 1: Two-Year Average Annual Return Above 13.6%	
1	1997-98	31.0%	1999
2	1975-76	30.5%	1977
3	1995-96	30.3%	1997
4	1996-97	28.2%	1998
5	1979-80	25.4%	1981
6	1985-86	25.3%	1987
7	1998-99	24.8%	2000
8	1988-89	24.2%	1990
9	1982-83	22.0%	1984
10	1994-95	19.4%	1996
11	2003-04	19.8%	2005
12	1984-85	19.2%	1986
13	1991-92	19.1%	1993
14	1971-72	16.6%	1973
15	1983-84	14.4%	1985
16	1989-90	14.2%	1991
17	1980-81	13.8%	1982
18	1990-91	13.7%	1992
		Tier 2: Two-Year Average Annual Return From 6.2% to 13.6%	
19	1978-79	12.5%	1980
20	1986-87	11.9%	1988
21	1987-88	11.0%	1989
22	1970-71	9.2%	1972
23	1992-93	8.8%	1994
24	1976-77	8.3%	1978
25	1981-82	8.3%	1983
26	2004-05	7.9%	2006
		Tier 3: Two-Year Average Annual Return Below 6.2%	
27	1999-00	6.0%	2001
28	1993-94	5.6%	1995
29	1974-75	5.4%	1976
30	2002-03	3.3%	2004
31	1972-73	2.2%	1974
32	1968-69	1.3%	1970
33	1977-78	−0.3%	1979
34	1969-70	−2.2%	1971
35	2000-01	−10.5%	2002
36	2001-02	−17.0%	2003
37	1973-74	−20.6%	1975

Step 2: Classify Each Year in Tier 1 and Tier 3 into Category A, B or C

Considering Tier 1 and Tier 3 together for the 1970-2006 period, there were sixteen category "A" years, one category "B" year and twelve category "C" years. Exhibit 10-2 (Panel 1) presents the details for classifying the category "A" years. Those classifications were established at the end of April. Of the category "A" years, twelve met condition 1 and four met condition 2.

Panel 2 of the exhibit presents the details for classifying 2001, the only category "B" year during 1970-2006. That classification was established on 02/21/01, the day the sell signal occurred. Panel 3 presents the details for classifying the twelve category "C" years during 1970-2006. Eight of those classifications were established at the end of January, the earliest it can occur. The classifications of the other four category "C" years were established between February 1st and February 11th. The day that each category "C" year's classification was established is a sell signal. Since the S&P 500 must fall before a sell signal can occur, none of those sell signals were at the exact top of a market cycle.

Exhibit 10-2

Establishing the Classifications of Category "A," "B" and "C" Years, 1970-2006

Panel 1: The Sixteen Category "A" Years

Year	Prior Year's December Low Date	Prior Year's December Low S&P 500	December Low Broken in January Date	December Low Broken in January S&P 500	January Change in S&P 500	Was December Low Broken in the February-through-April Period?
1971	12/01/70	87.47				No
1975	12/06/74	65.01				No
1976	12/05/75	86.82				No
1979	12/18/78	93.44				No
1985	12/13/84	161.81				No
1986	12/02/85	200.46				No
1987	12/31/86	242.17				No
1991	12/03/90	324.10	01/03/91	321.91	4.2%	No
1992	12/05/91	377.39				No
1993	12/02/92	429.89	01/08/93	429.05	0.7%	No
1995	12/08/94	445.45				No
1996	12/20/95	605.94	01/10/96	598.48	3.3%	No
1997	12/16/96	720.98				No
1998	12/24/97	932.70	01/09/98	927.69	1.0%	No
1999	12/14/98	1141.20				No
2004	12/10/03	1059.05				No

Panel 2: The One Category "B" Year

Year	Prior Year's December Low Date	Prior Year's December Low S&P 500	December Low Broken in the February-through-April Period Date	December Low Broken in the February-through-April Period S&P 500	January Change in S&P 500
2001	12/20/00	1264.74	02/21/01	1255.27	3.5%

Exhibit 10-2 continues on the next page.

Exhibit 10-2 (continued)

Panel 3: The Twelve Category "C" Years

Year	Prior Year's December Low		December Low Broken in the February-through-April Period		January Change in S&P 500
	Date	S&P 500	Date	S&P 500	
1970	12/17/69	89.20	01/23/70	89.07	−7.7%
1973	12/21/72	115.11	02/01/73	114.76	−1.7%
1974	12/05/73	92.16	02/11/74	90.66	−1.0%
1977	12/02/76	102.12	01/27/77	101.79	−5.1%
1981	12/11/80	127.36	02/02/81	126.91	−4.6%
1982	12/29/81	121.67	01/05/82	120.05	−1.8%
1984	12/15/83	161.67	02/03/84	160.91	−0.9%
1990	12/19/89	342.46	01/12/90	339.93	−6.9%
2000	12/01/99	1397.72	01/28/00	1360.16	−5.1%
2002	12/13/01	1119.38	01/22/02	1119.31	−1.6%
2003	12/27/02	875.40	01/24/03	861.40	−2.7%
2005	12/07/04	1177.07	01/20/05	1175.41	−2.5%

A line chart for each year during 1935-2006, along with a brief explanation of how that classification was established, is available at thewallstreettrafficlight.com. Go to the "Line Charts" and click on the year(s) you want to see.

Note that the three line charts in Chapter 8—for 1954, 1966 and 1969—are *not the same as* the charts for those years at the website. That is because the charts at the website have been prepared *as if the WSTL model were being used in real-time,* which is the approach described in Chapters 6 and 10. The charts in Chapter 8 were involved in *developing the model itself.*

Step 3: Calculate the Outcome of the Trade in Each 1B, 1C, 3B and 3C Year

Recall from the previous chapter how a (round-trip) trade was conducted. On the day of the sell signal (the day the classification of each 1B, 1C, 3B and 3C year was established), the S&P 500 was sold and the proceeds were put into 3-month T-bills. Then on the day of the buy signal, the S&P 500 was bought with the funds accumulated in the T-bills. From the sell signal to the buy signal, the WSTL was red.

Also recall that no S&P 500 dividends were received while the WSTL was red. This point is important because reinvested dividends accounted for just over 29% of the S&P 500's return for 1970-2006. The other 71% of the return was attributable to the S&P 500's mean price increase.

Exhibit 10-3 summarizes the 13 trades in category "B" and "C" years during 1970-2006. The mean profit per trade was 7.1%. Eleven of the trades were profitable. Note for 1973 that, even though the profit on the trade amounted to 11.7%, the WSTL return was a negative 3.0%; in other words, a profitable trade does not guarantee that the WSTL return for that year will be positive. There were two unprofitable trades: −18.4% in 2003 and −5.1% in 2005.

Exhibit 10-3

The Model's Thirteen Trades, 1970-2006

Year	Type of Year	WSTL Return	S&P 500 Return	Outcome of Trade
1970	3C	17.7%	4.0%	13.7%
1973	1C	−3.0%	−14.7%	11.7%
1974	3C	−16.0%	−26.5%	10.5%
1977	1C	4.5%	−7.2%	11.7%
1981	1C	13.1%	−4.9%	18.0%
1982	1C	39.8%	21.4%	18.4%
1984	1C	8.7%	6.3%	2.4%
1990	1C	2.1%	−3.2%	5.2%*
2000	1C	0.1%	−9.1%	9.2%
2001	3B	−6.3%	−11.9%	5.6%
2002	3C	−12.6%	−22.1%	9.5%
2003	3C	10.3%	28.7%	−18.4%
2005	1C	−0.2%	4.9%	−5.1%
Mean		4.5%	−2.6%	7.1%

*This difference does not add across due to rounding.

A Close Look at Selected Buy Signals

The previous chapter stated that if the lower limit for a buy signal were reached first, it would always trigger the buy signal on a day when the S&P 500 fell. As a result, it was possible that the buy signal could occur on or near (measured by number of trading days) the day of the S&P 500's lowest closing price during the year. The following table indicates that outcome did actually happen for three of the thirteen buy signals during 1970-2006:

Year	Type of Year	Buy Signal	Year's Low	Trading Days from Buy Signal to Year's Low
1970	3C	05/14/70	05/26/70	8
1977	1C	11/02/77	11/02/77	0
1981	1C	09/25/81	09/25/81	0

The extraordinary timing of those buy signals is a key factor in the WSTL strategy's superiority over buying-and-holding the S&P 500 during 1970-2006.

Appendices F and G

Appendix F presents the detailed calculations necessary to determine the WSTL return for each category "B" and "C" year in Exhibit 10-3. For easy reference, Appendix G presents a handy performance summary for the years in Tier 1, Tier 2 and Tier 3 from the entire 1935-2006 period. The years in each tier are in chronological order.

Chapter 11

◇◇◇◇◇◇◇◇◇◇◇◇◇◇◇◇

SIGNIFICANCE OF THE TEST RESULTS

Power Points

1. This book has told a David and Goliath story. "David" is the WSTL strategy, and "Goliath" is buying-and-holding the S&P 500 for the long-term.

2. The S&P 500's annual price changes during 1935-2006 fluctuated widely above and below the mean of 8.7% and *appear to be* random.

3. The efficient market theory, which has been developed by top scholars, leads to the conclusion that buy-and-hold is a wise investment strategy while any type of market timing is not a good strategy.

4. Four main groups of market timers are stock fund investors, stock fund managers, investment strategists at the largest Wall Street brokerage firms and investment newsletters. The historical performance of each group provides strong evidence that the stock market is efficient.

5. As described in previous chapters, the WSTL model was developed from S&P 500 data in 1935-1969 and then tested for 1970-2006. The test results indicated that the WSTL model achieved higher returns with lower risk than buying-and-holding the S&P 500.

6. The test results for 1970-2006 provide a strong challenge to the efficient market theory.

In the biblical account of David and Goliath, David used a sling and stone to kill Goliath. David's triumph defied logic because he was a young shepherd boy and Goliath was a nine-foot-tall champion warrior. Goliath was thought to be invincible. None of the observers that day knew David's weapon of choice until he used it.

Whether or not you realized it before this chapter, this book has described a classic confrontation between David and Goliath. "David" is the WSTL strategy. David challenges the leading scholars and professional money managers who say market timing—such as transferring money back and forth between the S&P 500 and a money market fund—is a loser's game that is utterly foolish to play. David's weapon of choice is the fundamental investment principle of returns reverting to the mean.

That weapon was the basis of the scientific test in which the WSTL model was developed from S&P 500 data in 1935-1969 and then tested for 1970-2006. The test results indicated the model achieved higher returns with lower risk. That means the *patterns in the S&P 500's annual returns and short-term movements incorporated in the model repeated themselves with a high degree of consistency during the entire 1935-2006 period.*

"Goliath" is buying-and-holding the S&P 500 for the long-term: for 35 years during 1935-1969 and for 37 years during 1970-2006. Today's conventional investing wisdom is to use the strategy of buying-and-holding the investor's target asset allocation. Most investors are familiar with this strategy through mutual fund materials, financial advisers and financial journalists. The rationale underlying the buy-and-hold strategy is the *efficient market theory*, discussed in the next section.

Previous chapters have fully explained the WSTL model and the accompanying investment strategy. This chapter describes Goliath's impressive résumé, provides a brief summary of David's victory for 1970-2006 and explains the significance of that victory.

Efficient Market Theory

A number of leading scholars have developed a body of knowledge called "modern portfolio theory." In 1990, three of those experts—Harry M. Markowitz, Merton H. Miller and William F. Sharpe—received the Nobel Prize in economics for their contributions to modern portfolio theory. Their research, along with research on modern portfolio theory by Paul A. Samuelson (also a Nobel laureate in economics), Eugene F. Fama, Fisher Black and others, dates back to the 1950s. A major tenet of modern portfolio theory is that financial markets are efficient.

In an **efficient financial market**, market prices incorporate all available information. As a result, market prices change only in response to "new information." That new information is often simply called "news." Examples of such news include reports on corporate earnings and dividends, earnings forecasts, the Federal Reserve's monetary policy (especially announcements of raising or lowering interest rates), the inflation rate, consumer spending, industrial production, the price of crude oil, major legislation (income taxes, the Sarbanes-Oxley Act and the like), U.S. Presidential and Congressional elections, and war and rumors of war. Such news tends to move the financial markets. The notion that financial markets are efficient is the basis of the efficient market theory.

Landmark statistical studies leading to the development of the **efficient market theory** found that stock prices, both individually and collectively, move in a random and unpredictable path through time—called the "random walk."[19] The random walk means that each item of new information will be random in regard to being better or worse than market participants had expected.[20] The random walk was popularized among investors by Burton Malkiel's long-time bestseller, *A Random Walk Down Wall Street.*

Exhibit 11-1 presents the S&P 500's annual price changes (no reinvested dividends are included) for 1935-2006. Those changes fluctuated widely above and below their mean of 8.7% and indeed *appear to be* random.[21]

Exhibit 11-1

S&P 500 Annual Price Changes, 1935-2006

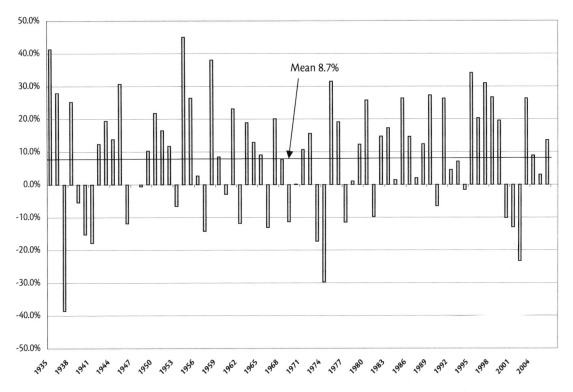

The efficient market theory holds that past stock prices are a completely unreliable source for forecasting future stock prices in any way that would produce returns (adjusted for risk) greater than the returns under the buy-and-hold strategy.[22] Under the efficient market theory, it would be impossible over the long-term for anyone to use the S&P 500's past annual returns and past daily closing prices to make forecasts that would achieve higher returns with lower risk than the S&P 500 itself. A "long-term" period virtually eliminates the element of luck in the forecasts, for the same reason that tossing a coin a large number of times is very unlikely to produce an abnormal percentage of either heads or tails. A period of, say, 30 years or more is generally regarded as the long-term. Scholars have found virtually no evidence that refutes the random walk of stock prices.[23]

Based on the efficient market theory, buy-and-hold is the wisest investment strategy. As a result, mutual fund companies urge investors to use that strategy and focus on the long-term performance of their portfolios—no matter how the financial markets move in the short-term. Mutual fund companies give investors a clear message: "Don't engage in market timing, and pay no attention to anyone who attempts to forecast the stock market." Said another way, market timing is a loser's game that is utterly foolish to play.

Performance of Market Timers

If the stock market were truly efficient, profitable market timing over the long-term would be impossible. A practical test of the validity of the efficient market theory is to determine whether anyone has used market timing to outperform, or "beat," the buy-and-hold strategy over the long-term. To perform this test, we will examine the historical record of four main groups of market timers: stock fund investors, stock fund managers, investment strategists at the largest Wall Street brokerage firms and investment newsletters.

1. **Market Timing by Stock Fund Investors**. Millions of mutual fund investors engage in market timing, transferring money back and forth between stock funds and money market funds. Dalbar Inc., a financial services research firm, studied market timing by stock fund investors from 1984 through 2002. The study found that those investors earned a mean annual return of 8.8% compared to the S&P 500's 13.5%.[24]

2. **Market Timing by Stock Fund Managers**. Most actively managed stock funds are run by managers who describe themselves as stock pickers, not market timers. Accordingly, their objective is to be fully invested in stocks, except for a "normal" percentage of fund assets—say 5%—held in cash. They maintain the cash cushion primarily to meet shareholders' redemptions that arise in the usual course of operations.

   When holding a higher-than-normal level of cash, mutual fund managers are in effect engaged in market timing. For example, a fund manager holding 12% cash—that is, more than double the 5% level—is forecasting a decline in the stock market. Goldman Sachs, a large Wall Street brokerage firm, studied mutual fund cash holdings from 1970 to 1989 and found that fund managers failed to call *all nine major turning points in the stock market during the 1970s and 1980s*.[25] Studies for other periods have reached the same conclusion. In a 1997 interview, John Bogle observed: "There is no evidence in the record of mutual fund managers showing that they have improved their performance by anticipating market changes and changing their cash positions."[26]

3. **Market Timing by Investment Strategists at the Largest Wall Street Brokerage Firms**. These strategists engage in market timing by changing the target asset allocation in their "model" (recommended) portfolios. For example, suppose a Merrill Lynch investment strategist advises an asset mix of 60% stocks, 35% bonds and 5% cash reserves. Then, a few months later he changes the allocation to 50% stocks, 35% bonds and 15% cash. The change—selling stocks and increasing cash, while leaving bonds unchanged—is a form of market timing. It would be profitable market timing if the stock market declines and the strategist then increased the model portfolio's asset allocation to stocks. On the other hand, it would be unprofitable market timing if the stock market rises and the strategist then increased the target asset allocation to stocks.

A study spanning 1987-1996 found that market timing by investment strategists at the largest Wall Street brokerage firms beat the buy-and-hold strategy by a mere 0.18%—despite the extensive resources available to them. That tiny gain, almost all of which came from timing the bond market rather than the stock market, actually would have been a loss if transaction costs were taken into account.[27]

4. **Market Timing by Investment Newsletters**. The leading tracker of investment newsletter performance is *Hulbert Financial Digest*. Its study for the 20 years ending June 30, 2000, found that *The Value Line Investment Survey* had the best performance (on a risk-adjusted basis) among the market timers—just slightly *below* what would have been achieved by buying-and-holding the S&P 500.[28]

Net of transaction costs, none of the four groups of market timers beat the strategy of simply buying-and-holding the S&P 500. *This single finding provides strong evidence that the stock market is efficient.*

Given the poor performance record of market timers, we can appreciate some humor from legendary investor Warren Buffett, a stock picker who disdains market timing. In the 1992 annual report of Berkshire Hathaway Corporation, he stated: "We've long felt that the only value of stock forecasters is to make fortune tellers look good....Short-term market forecasts are poison and should be kept locked up in a safe place, away from children and also from grown-ups who behave in the market like children."

Other Trappings of Goliath's Apparent Invincibility

To further enhance Goliath's résumé, here is an impressive list of testimonies that maintain it is impossible to be successful at market timing and short-term forecasting of the stock market:

- According to The Vanguard Group: "It is important to note that the bulk of major market movements—both up and down—often occur over brief periods....When stocks recover, it is common for the gains to be concentrated in a few days or weeks of extraordinary activity. Consequently, trying to time the markets by temporarily abandoning stocks requires a perfectly executed exit from the market, as well as an equally deft return—a nearly impossible feat. Be wary of self-proclaimed market seers promoting claims to the contrary."[29]

- John Bogle said: "After nearly fifty years in this business, I do not know of anybody who has done it [market timing] successfully and consistently. I don't even know anybody who *knows* anybody who has done it successfully and consistently."[30]

- Burton Malkiel said: "I have yet to see any compelling evidence that past stock prices can be used to predict future stock prices [well enough for any particular segment of the stock market to provide a higher average return while taking lower risk as compared to that segment]."[31]

- William Bernstein, a renowned financial adviser, said: "You are going to have to live with the markets the way they are—good years and bad years, occurring in a completely unpredictable sequence."[32]

- Peter Lynch, the top-performing mutual fund manager of all time, said: "I don't think anybody can predict whether the next 1,000 or 2,000 points in the [Dow Jones Industrial Average] will be up or down. You might as well flip a coin, which is what you're doing when you only have a one- or two-year horizon.... That's why...you should have a longer-term investment horizon when investing in the stock market."[33]

- Benjamin Graham, the father of security analysis, said: "If I have noticed anything over these 60 years on Wall Street, it is that people do not succeed in forecasting what's going to happen in the stock market."[34]

- T. Rowe Price, founder of the mutual fund company that bears his name, said: "History and experience have proven that correctly predicting the timing and extent of stock market trends is impossible because world developments and the psychological reactions of people are unpredictable."[35]

- Austin Pryor, editor of the *Sound Mind Investing* newsletter, said: "The investment world is a colossal engine fueled by human emotions. Each day millions of people make investing decisions reflecting their feelings of fear or security, hardship or prosperity. To attempt to make reliable forecasts in the face of this staggering complexity is foolhardy."[36]

Poking Fun at Short-Term Forecasts

Virtually no one has believed it is possible to use past prices (or any other historical data) to make short-term forecasts of the stock market that, over the long-term, achieve higher returns with lower risk than buying-and-holding the S&P 500. The general lack of success in making accurate short-term forecasts of the stock market over the years has led knowledgeable investors to use this analogy: forecasting the stock market based on past prices is like trying to drive a car by looking in the rearview mirror.

Because the vast majority of investors believe—and may have found out first-hand—that accurate short-term forecasting of the stock market is impossible, this story is told about Albert Einstein. When he died, Albert was warmly greeted by St. Peter at heaven's gate. In the conversation, St. Peter asked: "Would you be willing to stay in a dorm with three roommates until your plush cottage is ready next week?" Albert graciously agreed. St. Peter told Albert that one of his roommates has an IQ of 160, another's IQ is 120, but apologized for the third roommate's IQ being 100." Albert replied, "That's all right. I'll discuss higher mathematics with the first one. With the second, I'll talk about the upcoming NFL draft. I'll ask the third what he thinks the S&P 500 will do next year!"

David's Decisive Victory

The main message of this book is the powerful and simple nature of David's victory for 1970-2006. Exhibit 11-2 provides a brief summary of the WSTL model and its test results for that period. The forecast of the S&P 500 called for 1A, Tier 2 and 3A years to have the highest returns, and they did. Those years' mean returns were 21.0%, 18.2% and 23.7%, respectively—all far above 1970-2006's annual mean of 12.5%. Because the WSTL was green throughout those years, buying-and-holding the S&P 500 would have had the same returns as the WSTL.

Exhibit 11-2

A Brief Summary of the WSTL Model and Test Results

Type of Year	Forecast of the S&P 500 in Relation to Its Long-Term Mean	Model Tested for 1970-2006	
		WSTL Return	Number of Years
1A	Will not revert downward	21.0%	10
1B	Will revert downward	—	—
1C	Will revert downward	8.1%	8
Tier 2	Will revert upward	18.2%	8
3A	Will revert upward	23.7%	6
3B	Will not revert upward	−6.3%	1
3C	Will not revert upward	−0.2%	4
			37
Mean profit per trade		7.1%	13 trades

The distinguishing feature of the WSTL model is the success of the trades in 1B, 1C, 3B and 3C years. There were 13 trades during 1970-2006, and the mean profit per trade was 7.1%. That market-timing success resulted in the WSTL strategy achieving higher returns with lower risk than buy-and-hold. Exhibit 5-1 (p. 41) presents a summary of the returns and eight measures of risk under the two strategies for 1970-2006. David's victory was impressive indeed.

Significance of David's Victory

David's victory reveals that the patterns of the S&P 500's annual returns and short-term movements incorporated in the WSTL model were *not random* but repeated themselves with a high degree of consistency during 1935-2006. David's victory is significant because it refutes the validity of the efficient market theory's assertion that past movements in stock prices are not a reliable basis for forecasting their future movements in any way which makes returns (adjusted for risk) greater than they would be under the buy-and-hold strategy.

Specifically, the performance of the WSTL strategy for 1970-2006 refutes the efficient market theory on the following points:

- **Reversion to the mean**. Burton Malkiel said: "To be sure, we know in retrospect that stock prices tend to...revert to the mean. But it's never possible to know in advance when the reversion will occur."[37] However, the methodology on which Chapters 10 is based—classifying years into Tier 1, Tier 2 and Tier 3, and then classifying the years in Tier 1 and Tier 3 into the A, B and C categories—would have been an effective way to forecast when reversion to the mean was or was not going to occur.

- **Chart reading**. Malkiel also said: "It seems very clear that under scientific scrutiny chart reading must share a pedestal with alchemy."[38] However, the charts available at thewallstreettrafficlight.com demonstrate that, in more than 90% of the cases (that is, there were only five losing trades in 72 years), reading simple line charts would have been an effective way to classify 1A, 1B, 1C, 3A, 3B and 3C years throughout 1935-2006.

- **Large-cap stocks**. The efficient market theory maintains that the S&P 500 stocks— the largest U.S. companies as measured by total market value (large-cap stocks)—are the most efficient segment of the stock market. The rationale is simple: More information is available on those companies than smaller companies.[39] However, the WSTL's performance indicates that the large-cap segment of the stock market actually was not efficient.

Each of these points underscores the significance of David's victory for 1970-2006. When considered together, the points make a powerful case against the efficient market theory for that period.

The Real Test

Following publication of this book in December 2007, will the WSTL strategy achieve higher returns with lower risk than buying-and-holding the S&P 500? The correct answer is, time will tell. The results of that ongoing real-time test are updated quarterly at thewallstreettrafficlight.com.

What type of year was 2007? It was a Tier 2 year; the explanation for that classification appears on its chart at the website. What type of year will 2008 be? Check the website at the end of 2007 to see if it also is a Tier 2 year. If not, check again at the end of January 2008 to see the status of the year's forecast, which will be made between the end of January and the end of April.

A Call for Further Research

If you are a technical analyst, I hope you will be able to refine the WSTL model so that it achieves even better performance. One potentially fruitful area for research might be to incorporate trading volume in the model. For example, Charles Dow, a renowned technical analyst, recognized that the level of trading volume was a secondary (but important) factor in confirming price signals.[40]

Perhaps the WSTL model could be used—most likely in modified forms—to develop effective short-term forecasting models for other segments of the U.S. stock market. For example, given that small-cap stocks have achieved higher returns with higher risk than the S&P 500 over the years, that market segment is desirable for such research. Also, various forms of the research methodology might be useful in developing effective forecasting models for the bond market, commodity markets and financial markets in other countries. What unfound needles might there be in those financial-market haystacks?

Appendix A

◇◇◇◇◇◇◇◇◇◇◇◇◇◇◇

TOTAL ACCUMULATIONS FOR THE FAVORABLE AND UNFAVORABLE PARTS OF THE U.S. PRESIDENTIAL CYCLE, 1962-2006

Exhibit A-1

Total Accumulations for Favorable and Unfavorable Parts of the U.S. Presidential Cycle, 1962-2006

The "favorable part" of the cycle is October through December of years 1 and 2 plus all of years 3 and 4, a total of 30 months.

The "unfavorable part" of the cycle is January through September of years 1 and 2, a total of 18 months.

Panel 1: Total S&P 500 Accumulations for the Favorable and Unfavorable Parts

Year	S&P 500 Return for Favorable Part	S&P 500 Return for Unfavorable Part	Total Accumulation from One-Time Investment of $10,000 in the S&P 500	
			Favorable Part	**Unfavorable Part**
			$10,000	$10,000
1962	12.9%	−19.0%	$11,290	$8,096
1963	22.8%		$13,864	
1964	16.5%		$16,149	
1965	3.6%	8.7%	$16,728	$8,800
1966	5.7%	−14.9%	$17,677	$7,490
1967	24.0%		$21,916	
1968	11.1%		$24,340	
1969	−0.4%	−8.2%	$24,235	$6,876
1970	10.4%	−5.6%	$26,754	$6,492
1971	14.3%		$30,584	

Exhibit A-1 continues on the next page.

Exhibit A-1: Panel 1 (continued)

Year	S&P 500 Return for Favorable Part	S&P 500 Return for Unfavorable Part	Total Accumulation from One-Time Investment of $10,000 in the S&P 500	
			Favorable Part	Unfavorable Part
1973	−9.4%	−6.1%	$32,980	$6,095
1974	8.7%	−32.4%	$35,850	$4,119
1975	37.2%		$49,188	
1976	23.8%		$60,916	
1977	−0.4%	−6.9%	$60,664	$3,834
1978	−4.9%	12.0%	$57,686	$4,293
1979	18.4%		$68,323	
1980	32.4%		$90,472	
1981	6.7%	−10.8%	$96,513	$3,829
1982	18.4%	3.3%	$114,306	$3,954
1983	22.5%		$140,041	
1984	6.3%		$148,816	
1985	17.5%	13.3%	$174,827	$4,479
1987	5.2%		$194,354	
1988	16.8%		$227,024	
1989	2.3%	28.9%	$232,170	$6,488
1990	8.7%	−10.9%	$252,451	$5,784
1991	30.5%		$329,574	
1992	7.7%		$354,838	
1993	2.4%	7.5%	$363,230	$6,220
1994	−0.0%	1.3%	$363,089	$6,304
1995	37.4%		$499,005	
1996	23.1%		$614,146	
1997	3.0%	29.7%	$632,730	$8,173
1998	21.3%	6.2%	$767,719	$8,683
1999	21.0%		$929,235	
2000	−9.1%		$844,561	
2001	10.6%	−20.3%	$933,877	$6,920
2002	8.2%	−28.0%	$1,010,728	$4,980
2003	28.7%		$1,300,808	
2004	10.9%		$1,442,205	
2005	2.1%	2.8%	$1,471,886	$5,121
2006	6.7%	8.6%	$1,570,637	$5,564
CAGR			19.99%	−3.34%

Exhibit A-1 (continued)

Panel 2: Total T-Bill Accumulation for the Unfavorable Part

Year	3-Month T-Bill Return for Unfavorable Part	Total Accumulation from One-Time Investment of $10,000 in 3-Month T-bills for Unfavorable Part
		$10,000
1962	2.07%	$10,207
1963		
1964		
1965	2.91%	$10,504
1966	4.48%	$10,975
1967		
1968		
1969	4.83%	$11,505
1970	5.06%	$12,087
1971		
1972		
1973	5.16%	$12,710
1974	5.99%	$13,472
1975		
1976		
1977	3.74%	$13,976
1978	5.05%	$14,681
1979		
1980		
1981	11.09%	$16,310
1982	8.64%	$17,719
1983		
1984		
1985	5.69%	$18,727
1986	4.64%	$19,596
1987		
1988		
1989	6.20%	$20,811
1990	5.75%	$22,008
1991		
1992		
1993	2.24%	$22,500
1994	2.93%	$23,160

Exhibit A-1 continues on the next page.

Exhibit A-1: Panel 2 (continued)

Year	3-Month T-Bill Return for Unfavorable Part	Total Accumulation from One-Time Investment of $10,000 in 3-Month T-bills for Unfavorable Part
1995		
1996		
1997	3.79%	$24,037
1998	3.71%	$24,929
1999		
2000		
2001	2.91%	$25,655
2002	1.27%	$25,981
2003		
2004		
2005	2.19%	$26,550
2006	3.50%	$27,479
CAGR		6.04%

Appendix B

◇◇◇◇◇◇◇◇◇◇◇◇◇

S&P 500 DECLINES OF 10% OR MORE, 1935-2006

Exhibit B-1

Declines of 10% or More in the S&P 500, 1935-2006

Each decline occurred without an intervening advance of at least 5%.
The dividing line separates the sample period from the test period.

Row	Ending Date	Type of Year	Decline of 10% or More	Number of Trading Days
1	03/14/35	1C	13.7%	20
2	04/29/36	1A	12.8%	19
3	06/28/37	1B	19.1%	94
4	09/25/37	1B	24.4%	35
5	10/18/37	1B	21.8%	12
6	11/08/37	1B	10.0%	6
7	11/24/37	1B	15.0%	11
8	02/03/38	3B	13.5%	20
9	03/31/38	3B	27.2%	31
10	05/31/38	3B	12.8%	18
11	09/27/38	3B	12.9%	27
12	12/09/38	3B	10.7%	24
13	01/26/39	3C	12.8%	19
14	04/08/39	3C	22.3%	24
15	08/24/39	3C	11.2%	28
16	06/10/40	1C	31.9%	187
17	02/14/41	3C	16.4%	78
18	12/29/41	3C	20.1%	126
19	04/28/42	3B	17.8%	94
20	11/29/43	3A	10.2%	55

Exhibit B-1 continues on the next page.

Exhibit B-1 (continued)

Row	Ending Date	Type of Year	Decline of 10% or More	Number of Trading Days
21	02/26/46	1B	10.2%	17
22	09/19/46	1B	25.6%	78
23	04/18/47	1B	13.0%	56
24	03/16/48	3C	12.3%	119
25	09/27/48	3C	11.0%	72
26	11/30/48	3C	11.7%	22
27	06/13/49	3B	11.0%	60
28	07/17/50	Tier 2	14.0%	24
29	06/10/53	1C	11.7%	109
30	10/11/55	1A	10.6%	12
31	10/01/56	1C	10.1%	41
32	10/22/57	1C	20.7%	70
33	03/08/60	1C	11.5%	44
34	05/28/62	1C	23.6%	115
35	06/26/62	1C	12.3%	18
36	10/23/62	1C	10.5%	43
37	08/29/66	1B	19.4%	90
38	07/29/69	1C	15.7%	51
39	01/30/70	3C	13.5%	56
40	05/26/70	3C	23.2%	59
41	08/09/71	3A	10.7%	71
42	11/23/71	3A	11.0%	54
43	05/21/73	1C	14.6%	89
44	12/05/73	1C	17.3%	37
45	05/29/74	3C	12.9%	53
46	07/11/74	3C	14.2%	22
47	09/13/74	3C	21.1%	26
48	10/03/74	3C	11.2%	9
49	12/06/74	3C	13.6%	20
50	09/16/75	3A	14.1%	44
51	05/31/77	1C	10.6%	104
52	11/02/77	1C	10.9%	75
53	03/06/78	Tier 2	10.1%	68
54	11/14/78	Tier 2	13.6%	45
55	11/07/79	3A	10.2%	23
56	03/27/80	Tier 2	17.1%	30
57	09/25/81	1C	15.7%	32
58	03/08/82	1C	15.0%	67

Exhibit B-1 (continued)

Row	Ending Date	Type of Year	Decline of 10% or More	Number of Trading Days
59	08/12/82	1C	14.2%	65
60	07/24/84	1C	14.4%	199
61	10/19/87	1A	31.5%	10
62	10/26/87	1A	11.9%	3
63	12/04/87	1A	12.4%	23
64	01/30/90	1C	10.2%	20
65	08/23/90	1C	16.8%	28
66	10/27/97	1A	10.8%	14
67	08/31/98	1A	19.3%	31
68	10/08/98	1A	10.0%	11
69	04/14/00	1C	11.2%	15
70	10/12/00	1C	12.6%	28
71	12/20/00	1C	11.7%	31
72	03/22/01	3B	18.6%	36
73	09/21/01	3B	26.4%	82
74	05/07/02	3C	10.3%	34
75	07/23/02	3C	27.9%	45
76	10/09/02	3C	19.3%	33
77	03/11/03	3C	14.1%	38

Appendix C

◇◇◇◇◇◇◇◇◇◇◇◇◇◇◇

SETTING THE LIMITS FOR BUY SIGNALS

Chapter 8 illustrated how to use the line chart to establish the classifications of category "B" years during the February-through-April period, and the classifications of category "C" years between the end of January and the end of April. The particular day when each of those classifications was established is a sell signal, the day the WSTL turns from green to red.

Following each sell signal, later in the year the buy signal—the day the WSTL turns from red to green—is triggered by *whichever of three limits is reached first*: (1) the lower limit for the S&P 500's closing price, (2) the upper limit for the S&P 500's closing price or (3) the time limit. The upper limit serves as a "stop loss" because it confines the size of an unprofitable trade.

The specifications of the three limits for category "B" years are not the same as those for category "C" years. That's because the S&P 500's short-term movements tended to have a different pattern in each of those categories of years during 1935-1969.

This appendix applies 20/20 hindsight to the 1935-1969 sample period to set the three limits for category "B" years and the three limits for category "C" years—which then were used during the 1970-2006 test period. Those limits were set such that they *maximized the total profitability of the trades during 1935-1969* under step 2 of the four-step process used to develop the WSTL model.41

The Three Limits for Buy Signals in Category "B" Years

The lower limit for a category "B" year is the S&P 500 closing (for the first time after the sell signal) *at least 10.38% below the prior year's closing price*. As a result, the buy signals in 1947 and 1949 each occurred on the day of the S&P 500's low for the year while the buy signals in 1938 and 1942 each occurred shortly before the year's low.

- The lower limit in 1947 was 13.71. To calculate it, multiply 15.30 (the S&P 500's closing price at the end of 1946) by 89.62% (100% minus the lower limit of 10.38%): 15.30 × 0.8962 = 13.71. For 1947, the S&P 500's only closing price at or below 13.71 was 13.71 on 05/17/47. That was the day of the buy signal.

- The lower limit in 1949 was 13.62: 15.20 (the S&P 500's closing price at the end of 1948) × 89.62% = 13.62. For 1949, the S&P 500's only closing price at or below 13.62 was 13.55 on 06/13/49. That was the day of the buy signal.

- The lower limit in 1938 was 9.45: 10.55 (the S&P 500's closing price at the end of 1937) × 89.62% = 9.45. For 1938, the S&P 500's first closing price at or below 9.45 was 9.35 on 03/25/38. That was the day of the buy signal, which occurred five trading days before the low for the year, on 03/31/38.

- The lower limit in 1942 was 7.79: 8.69 (the S&P 500's closing price at the end of 1941) × 89.62% = 7.79. For 1942, the S&P 500's first closing price at or below 7.79 was 7.70 on 04/17/42. That was the day of the buy signal, which occurred nine trading days before the low for the year, on 04/28/42.

The upper limit for category "B" years is the S&P 500 closing (for the first time after the sell signal) *at least 13.85% above its closing price on the day of the sell signal*. The upper limit was set by adding 0.01% to the S&P 500's maximum rise between the sell signal and buy signal of 13.84%, which occurred in 1946 (see the shaded area in Exhibit C-1). As a result, none of the trades in the category "B" years during 1935-1969 were triggered by the upper limit.

Exhibit C-1

Setting the Upper Limit for Buy Signals in "B" Years

	Sell Signal		S&P 500 Peak Between the Sell Signal and Buy Signal			
Year	Date	S&P 500 Closing Price	Date	Closing Price	Rise from Sell Signal*	Outcome of Trade
1937	04/26/37	16.16	05/04/37	16.73	3.53%	3.0%
1938	03/18/38	10.19	03/19/38	10.41	2.16%	11.5%
1942	03/06/42	8.16	03/17/42	8.29	1.59%	5.9%
1946	02/25/46	16.91	05/29/46	19.25	13.84%	9.4%
1947	04/14/47	14.14	05/05/47	14.85	5.02%	2.6%
1949	02/05/49	14.85	03/29/49	15.22	2.49%	8.3%
1966	03/01/66	90.06	04/21/66	92.42	2.62%	8.8%

*Maximum heat taken

The next-to-last column in Exhibit C-1 shows that, following the rise of 13.84% in 1946, the next largest rise was 5.02% in 1947. Given that 1946's percentage is so much greater than the one in 1947, why not use a smaller percentage for the upper limit in category "B" years? Because the trade in 1946 would have been unprofitable *if the upper limit had been set lower than 13.85%*. Certainly, the investor would have taken considerable "heat" when, between a sell signal and a buy signal, the S&P 500 rose by such a large percentage.

The buy signal on 09/03/46 was the latest calendar date that a buy signal occurred in any of the category "B" years during 1935-1969. *The end of September was chosen as the time limit* because, in four of the seven category "B" years, the S&P 500's closing price was lower at the end of September than at the end of October, November or December.

To illustrate the three limits for a category "B" year, consider 1937—the first category "B" year during 1935-1969. Its three limits are as follows:

Event	S&P 500	Limit	S&P 500
End of the prior year (1936)	17.18	Lower: 17.18 × (100% − 10.38%) =	15.40
Sell signal on 04/26/37	16.16	Upper: 16.16 × (100% + 13.85%) =	18.40
End of September 1937	13.76	Time:	13.76

The lower limit was reached first, on 06/14/37. The S&P 500's closing price that day was 15.20. From the sell signal to the buy signal, the S&P 500 fell 0.96 points (from 16.16 to 15.20), or 5.94% (0.96 ÷ 16.16).

All of the buy signals in category "B" years during 1935-1969 were triggered by the lower limit. Therefore, all of those trades were profitable (see Panel 1 of Exhibit 9-1, p. 77). Appendix D calculates the WSTL's returns for each of the category "B" years during 1935-1969.

The Three Limits for Buy Signals in Category "C" Years

The lower limit for a category "C" year is the S&P 500 closing (for the first time after the sell signal) *at least 10.93% below the closing price on the day of the sell signal*. As a result, the buy signals in 1935 and 1953 each occurred on the day of the S&P 500's low for the year, while the buy signals in 1939 and 1957 each occurred one trading day before the year's low.

- The lower limit in 1935 was 8.11. To calculate it, multiply 9.10 (the S&P 500's closing price on the day of the sell signal) by 89.07% (100% minus the lower limit of 10.93%): 9.10 × 89.07% = 8.11. For 1935, the S&P 500's only closing price at or below 8.11 was 8.06, on 03/14/35. That was the day of the buy signal.

- The lower limit in 1953 was 22.71: 25.50 (the S&P 500's closing price on the day of the sell signal) × 89.07% = 22.71. For 1953, the S&P 500's only closing price at or below 22.71 was 22.71, on 09/14/53. That was the day of the buy signal.

- The lower limit in 1939 was 10.96: 12.30 (the S&P 500's closing price on the day of the sell signal) × 89.07%. For 1939, the S&P 500's first closing price at or below 10.96 was 10.66 on 04/06/39. That was the day of the buy signal, which occurred one trading day before the low for the year, on 04/08/39.

- The lower limit in 1957 was 39.83: 44.72 (the S&P 500's closing price on the day of the sell signal) × 89.07%. For 1957, the S&P 500's first closing price at or below 39.83

was 39.15 on 10/21/57. That was the day of the buy signal, which occurred one trading day before the low for the year, on 10/22/57.

The upper limit for category "C" years is the S&P 500 closing (for the first time after the sell signal) *at least 16.14% above its closing price on the day of the sell signal.* The upper limit was set by adding 0.01% to the S&P 500's maximum rise between the sell signal and buy signal of 16.13%, which occurred in 1948 (see the shaded area in Exhibit C-2). Setting the upper limit at 16.14% prevented the trade in 1948 from having had a loss of approximately that size. Instead, 1948's trade—triggered by the time limit—lost 4.7% (shown in Panel 2 of Exhibit 9-1, p. 77). The buy signal in 1968 was the only one triggered by the upper limit in a category "C" year during 1935-1969.

Exhibit C-2

Setting the Upper Limit for Buy Signals in "C" Years

	Sell Signal		S&P 500 Peak Between the Sell Signal and Buy Signal			
Year	Date	S&P 500 Closing Price	Date	Closing Price	Rise from Sell Signal*	Outcome of Trade
1935	End 1/35	9.10	02/18/35	9.34	2.64%	17.7%
1939	End 1/39	12.30	03/10/39	13.10	6.50%	13.5%
1940	End 1/40	12.05	04/08/40	12.59	4.48%	12.9%
1941	End 1/41	10.07	07/28/41	10.47	3.97%	3.6%
1948	End 1/48	14.69	06/15/48	17.06	16.13%	−4.7%
1953	02/17/53	25.50	03/17/53	26.33	3.25%	9.5%
1956	End 1/56	43.82	08/02/56	49.74	13.51%	−4.0%
1957	End 1/57	44.72	07/15/57	49.13	9.86%	11.9%
1960	End 1/60	55.61	08/24/60	58.07	4.42%	−0.5%
1962	End 1/62	68.84	03/15/62	71.06	3.22%	11.0%
1968	End 1/68	92.24	11/26/68	107.26	16.28%	−13.8%
1969	End 1/69	103.01	05/14/69	106.16	3.06%	14.3%

*Maximum heat taken

An obvious question is, why wasn't the upper limit for a category "C" year set at 16.29% to accommodate 1968's maximum rise of 16.28%? Because that rise (to 107.26) was on 11/26/68 while the high for 1968 (108.37) was on the last trading day of November, which—as explained below—was the time limit for buy signals in category "C" years. That means the trade in 1968 would have been more unprofitable (by approximately one percentage point) had the upper limit been set at 16.29%.

The end of November was chosen as the time limit for category "C" years. That's because, for three of the four years during the sample period in which the lower or upper limit did not trigger a buy signal by the end of October, the S&P 500's closing price was lower at the end of November than at the end of October or December. Setting the time limit for category "C" years at the end of November maximized the profitability of the trades for those four years.

To illustrate the three limits for a category "C" year, consider 1935. Its three limits are as follows:

Event	S&P 500	Limit	S&P 500
Sell signal, end of January 1935	9.10	Lower: 9.10 × (100% − 10.93%) =	8.11
		Upper: 9.10 × (100% + 16.14%) =	10.57
End of November 1935	12.95	Time:	12.95

The lower limit was reached first, on 03/14/35. The S&P 500's closing price that day was 8.06. From the sell signal to the buy signal, the S&P fell 1.04 points (from 9.10 to 8.06), or 11.4% (1.04 ÷ 9.10).

Consider another category "C" year, 1968. Its three limits are as follows:

Event	S&P 500	Limit	S&P 500
Sell signal, end of January 1968	92.24	Lower: 92.24 × (100% − 10.93%) =	82.16
		Upper: 92.24 × (100% + 16.14%) =	107.13
End of November 1968	108.37	Time:	108.37

The upper limit was reached first, on 11/26/68. The S&P 500's closing price that day was 107.26. From the sell signal to the buy signal, the S&P 500 rose 15.02 points (from 92.24 to 107.26), or 16.28% (15.02 ÷ 92.24).

Consider another category "C" year, 1948. Its three limits are as follows:

Event	S&P 500	Limit	S&P 500
Sell signal, end of January 1948	14.69	Lower: 14.69 × (100% − 10.93%) =	13.08
		Upper: 14.69 × (100% + 16.14%) =	17.06
End of November 1948	14.75	Time:	14.75

The time limit was reached first, at the end of November 1948. The S&P 500's closing price that day was 14.75. From the sell signal to the buy signal, the S&P 500 rose 0.06 points (from 14.69 to 14.76), or 0.41% (0.06 ÷ 14.69).

Appendix D calculates the WSTL's returns for each category "C" year during 1935-1969.

Summary

This appendix has explained how the limits for buy signals in category "B" and "C" years were set based on the S&P 500's short-term movements during 1935-1969. Exhibit C-3 summarizes the specifications for those limits.

Exhibit C-3

The Limits for Buy Signals

Type of Limit	Specification of the Limit
	Category "B" Year
Lower	• The S&P 500 closes, for the first time after the sell signal, at least 10.38% below the prior year's closing price.
Upper	• The S&P 500 closes, for the first time after the sell signal, at least 13.85% above its closing price on the day of the sell signal.
Time	• The end of September.
	Category "C" Year
Lower	• The S&P 500 closes, for the first time after the sell signal, at least 10.93% below its closing price on the day of the sell signal.
Upper	• The S&P 500 closes, for the first time after the sell signal, at least 16.14% above its closing price on the day of the sell signal.
Time	• The end of November.

CALCULATING THE RETURNS FOR CATEGORY B AND C YEARS, 1935-1969

For a category "B" or "C" year, the WSTL return relative to the buy-and-hold return was primarily governed by *the change in the S&P 500 while the WSTL was red*. A negative change in the S&P 500 increases the WSTL return relative to the S&P 500 return. A positive change has the opposite effect. Also, for that time between a sell signal and a buy signal, the WSTL strategy earns interest on 3-month T-bills but the S&P 500's dividends are forgone.

Appendix C explained how the lower limits, upper limits and time limits were set for the buy signals in category "B" and "C" years. The outcome of each trade depends on which limit was reached first. Regardless of which limit was reached first, a seven-step procedure is used to calculate the WSTL return for each year with a trade.

Calculating the WSTL Returns for Category "B" Years

Appendix C specified the three limits to determine the buy signal in each category "B" year:

Lower limit: The S&P 500 closes, for the first time after the sell signal, at least 10.38% below the prior year's closing price.

Upper limit: The S&P 500 closes, for the first time after the sell signal, at least 13.85% above its closing price on the day of the sell signal.

Time limit: The end of September.

Exhibit D-1 indicates that the lower limit triggered the buy signal in each of the seven category "B" years during 1935-1969. All of those trades were profitable. The mean profit per trade was 7.1%.

Exhibit D-1

Trades in Category "B" Years, 1935-1969

Year	Trigger for Buy Signal	WSTL Return	S&P 500 Return	Outcome of Trade
1937	Lower limit	−32.0%	−35.0%	3.0%
1938	Lower limit	42.7%	31.1%	11.5%*
1942	Lower limit	26.2%	20.3%	5.9%
1946	Lower limit	1.3%	−8.1%	9.4%
1947	Lower limit	8.3%	5.7%	2.6%
1949	Lower limit	27.0%	18.8%	8.3%*
1966	Lower limit	−1.3%	−10.1%	8.8%
Mean		10.3%	3.2%	7.1%

*This difference does not add across due to rounding.

1942 is used to illustrate the seven-step procedure, which calculated the WSTL return to be 26.2%. 1942 was a category "B" year because the December 1941 low was broken on 03/06/42 and January's change was positive. That day was the sell signal. The lower limit was 10.38% below the S&P 500 closing price at the end of 1941: 8.69 × (100% − 10.38%) = 7.79. The first S&P 500 closing price at or below 7.79 was on 04/17/42, the day of the buy signal:

Date	S&P 500	Signal
03/06/42	8.16	Sell
03/07/42	8.23	
03/09/42	8.20	
03/10/42	8.14	
03/11/42	7.98	
03/12/42	7.98	
03/13/42	8.03	
03/14/42	8.02	
03/16/42	8.12	
03/17/42	8.29	
03/18/42	8.21	
03/19/42	8.20	
03/20/42	8.11	
03/21/42	8.12	
03/23/42	8.15	
03/24/42	8.22	
03/25/42	8.16	
03/26/42	8.13	
03/27/42	8.05	
03/28/42	8.05	
03/30/42	8.06	
03/31/42	8.01	
04/01/42	8.05	
04/02/42	8.11	
04/04/42	8.11	
04/06/42	8.20	
04/07/42	8.16	
04/08/42	8.12	
04/09/42	7.99	
04/10/42	7.98	
04/11/42	7.96	
04/13/42	7.96	
04/14/42	7.83	
04/15/42	7.81	
04/16/42	7.82	
04/17/42	7.70	Buy

Exhibit D-2 applies the seven steps to 1942. The details of each step are as follows.

Step 1: On the day of the sell signal, calculate the total value of the WSTL's investment in the S&P 500:

$$8.16 + (8.69 \times 7.91\%) \times (65 \div 365) = 8.28$$

- 8.16 is the S&P 500 closing price on the day of the sell signal, 03/06/42.

- 8.69 is the S&P 500 closing price at the end of 1941.

- 7.91% is the S&P 500 dividend yield for 1942.

- 65 is the number of days from the beginning of the year to the day of the sell signal, which is used to prorate the S&P 500 dividends for 1942.

Step 2: On the day of the buy signal, calculate the interest earned while the WSTL was red (measured in terms of the WSTL's investment in the S&P 500 on the day of the sell signal):

$$8.28 \times 0.28\% \times (42 \div 365) = 0.00$$

- 8.28 is the answer from step 1.

- 0.28% is the average annual interest rate on 3-month T-bills from the day of the sell signal to the day of the buy signal (that is, the period when the WSTL was red).

- 42 is the number of days the WSTL was red.

Step 3: On the day of the buy signal, calculate the total value of the WSTL's investment in 3-month T-bills (measured in terms of the S&P 500 closing price on that day):

$$8.28 + 0.00 = 8.28$$

- 8.28 is the answer from step 1, and 0.00 is the answer from step 2.

Step 4: At year-end, calculate the total value of the WSTL's investment in the S&P 500 (not including dividends earned since the day of the buy signal):

$$8.28 \times (9.77 \div 7.70) = 10.51$$

- 8.28 is the answer from step 3.

- 9.77 is the S&P 500 closing price at the end of 1942.

- 7.70 is the S&P 500 closing price on the day of the buy signal.

Step 5: At year-end, calculate the dividends earned since the day of the buy signal:

$$8.28 \times 7.91\% \times (258 \div 365) = 0.46$$

- 8.28 is the answer from step 3.

- 7.91% is the S&P 500 dividend yield for 1942.

- 258 is the number of days from the buy signal to the end of 1942, which is used to prorate the S&P 500 dividends for 1942.

Step 6: At year-end, calculate the total value of the WSTL's investment in the S&P 500:

10.51 + 0.46 = 10.97

• 10.51 is the answer from step 4, and 0.46 is the answer from step 5.

Step 7: At year-end, calculate the WSTL annual return:

(10.97 ÷ 8.69) − 1.00 = 26.24%

• 10.97 is the answer from step 6.

• 8.69 is the S&P 500 closing price at the end of 1941.

The WSTL return of 26.2% for 1942 was *5.9% greater than the S&P 500 return of 20.3%*. In other words, the trade in 1942 had a profit of 5.9% (26.2% − 20.3%). The "1942" row of Exhibit D-1 shows those three percentages. Exhibit D-4 calculates the WSTL returns for the seven category "B" years listed in Exhibit D-1.

Exhibit D-2

Calculating the WSTL Return for 1942

Step 1:	Total value of the WSTL's investment in the S&P 500 at the sell signal, 03/06/42 S&P 500 closing price + year-to-date dividend earned 8.16 + (8.69 × 7.91%) × (65 ÷ 365) =	8.28
Step 2:	The buy signal was triggered by the lower limit on 04/17/42. Add: Interest earned while WSTL was red (measured in terms of the WSTL's investment in the S&P 500 at the sell signal) 8.28 × 0.28% × (42 ÷ 365) =	0.00
Step 3:	Total value of the WSTL's investment in 3-month T-bills (measured in terms of the S&P 500 closing price on the day of the buy signal)	8.28
	Year-end 1942	
Step 4:	Total value of the WSTL's investment in the S&P 500 at year-end (not including dividends earned since the buy signal) Total value from step 3 × Percentage change in S&P 500 since the buy signal 8.28 × (9.77 ÷ 7.70) =	10.51
Step 5:	Add: Dividends earned since the buy signal 8.28 × 7.91% × (258 ÷ 365) =	0.46
Step 6:	Total value of the WSTL's investment in the S&P 500	10.97
Step 7:	WSTL annual return Total value from step 6 ÷ S&P 500 closing price at the end of 1941 (10.97 ÷ 8.69) − 1.00 =	26.24%

Calculating the WSTL Returns for Category "C" Years

Appendix C specified the three limits to determine the buy signal in each category "C" year:

Lower limit: The S&P 500 closes, for the first time after the sell signal, at least 10.93% below the closing price on the day of the sell signal.

Upper limit: The S&P 500 closes, for the first time after the sell signal, at least 16.14% above its closing price on the day of the sell signal.

Time limit: The end of November.

Exhibit D-3 indicates which limit triggered the buy signal in each of the 12 category "C" years during 1935-1969. Eight of those trades were profitable and four were unprofitable. The mean profit per trade was 6.0%.

Exhibit D-3

Trades in Category "C" Years, 1935-1969

Year	Trigger for Buy Signal	WSTL Return	S&P 500 Return	Outcome of Trade
1935	Lower limit	65.4%	47.7%	17.7%
1939	Lower limit	13.1%	−0.4%	13.5%
1940	Lower limit	3.1%	−9.8%	12.9%
1941	Time limit	−8.0%	−11.6%	3.6%
1948	Time limit	0.9%	5.5%	−4.7%*
1953	Lower limit	8.5%	−1.0%	9.5%
1956	Time limit	2.6%	6.6%	−4.0%
1957	Lower limit	1.2%	−10.8%	11.9%*
1960	Time limit	0.0%	0.5%	−0.5%
1962	Lower limit	2.3%	−8.7%	11.0%
1968	Upper limit	−2.8%	11.1%	−13.8%*
1969	Lower limit	5.8%	−8.5%	14.3%
Mean		7.7%	1.7%	6.0%

*This difference does not add across due to rounding.

Although the three limits are different for category "C" years than for category "B" years, the same seven-step procedure illustrated in Exhibit D-2 is suitable to calculate the WSTL returns for category "C" years. Exhibit D-5 uses that procedure to calculate the WSTL returns for the 12 category "C" years listed in Exhibit D-3.

Exhibit D-4

Details of WSTL Trades and Returns for Category "B" Years, 1935-1969

Panel 1: Basic Data for Trades in Category "B" Years

Year	Sell Signal	Buy Signal	S&P 500 Closing Price				S&P 500 Annual Dividend Yield*	Average Annual Rate on 3-mo. T-Bills#	Three Segments of Year (calendar days)		
			End of Prior Year	Sell Signal	Buy Signal	End of Year			Start of Year to Sell Signal (Green Light)	Sell Signal to Buy Signal (Red Light)	Buy Signal to Year-End (Green Light)
1937	04/26/37	06/14/37	17.18	16.16	15.20	10.55	3.57%	0.38%	116	49	200
1938	03/18/38	03/25/38	10.55	10.19	9.35	13.21	5.91%	0.08%	77	7	281
1942	03/06/42	04/17/42	8.69	8.16	7.70	9.77	7.91%	0.28%	65	42	258
1946	02/25/46	09/03/46	17.36	16.91	15.00	15.30	3.80%	0.38%	56	190	119
1947	04/14/47	05/17/47	15.30	14.14	13.71	15.30	5.71%	0.38%	104	33	228
1949	02/05/49	06/13/49	15.20	14.85	13.55	16.76	8.53%	1.17%	36	128	201
1966	03/01/66	08/01/66	92.43	90.06	82.31	80.33	3.03%	4.63%	60	153	152

*assumed to be evenly distributed during the year.

#while the WSTL was red.

Exhibit D-4, Panel 2: Calculating the WSTL Returns for Category "B" Years

---

1937

Step 1:   Total value of the WSTL's investment in the S&P 500 at the sell signal, 4/26/37
S&P 500 closing price + year-to-date dividend earned
16.16 + (17.18 × 3.57%) × (116 ÷ 365) =   16.35

Step 2:   The buy signal was triggered by the lower limit on 6/14/37.
Add: Interest earned while WSTL was red (measured in terms of the WSTL's
investment in the S&P 500 at the sell signal)
16.35 × 0.38% × (49 ÷ 365) =   0.01

Step 3:   Total value of the WSTL's investment in 3-month T-bills (measured in terms of
the S&P 500 closing price on the day of the buy signal)   16.36

Year-end 1937

Step 4:   Total value of the WSTL's investment in the S&P 500 at year-end (not including
dividends earned since the buy signal)
Total value from step 3 × Percentage change in S&P 500 since the buy signal
16.36 × (10.55 ÷ 15.20) =   11.36

Step 5:   Add: Dividends earned since the buy signal
16.36 × 3.57% × (200 ÷ 365) =   0.32

Step 6:   Total value of the WSTL's investment in the S&P 500   11.68

Step 7:   WSTL annual return
Total value from step 6 ÷ S&P 500 closing price at the end of 1936
(11.68 ÷ 17.18) − 1.00 =   −32.01%

1938

Step 1:   Total value of the WSTL's investment in the S&P 500 at the sell signal, 3/18/38
S&P 500 closing price + year-to-date dividend earned
10.19 + (10.55 × 5.91%) × (77 ÷ 365) =   10.32

Step 2:   The buy signal was triggered by the lower limit on 3/25/38.
Add: Interest earned while WSTL was red (measured in terms of the WSTL's
investment in the S&P 500 at the sell signal)
10.32 × 0.08% × (7 ÷ 365) =   0.00

Step 3:   Total value of the WSTL's investment in 3-month T-bills (measured in terms of
the S&P 500 closing price on the day of the buy signal)   10.32

Year-end 1938

Step 4:   Total value of the WSTL's investment in the S&P 500 at year-end (not including
dividends earned since the buy signal)
Total value from step 3 × Percentage change in S&P 500 since the buy signal
10.32 × (13.21 ÷ 9.35) =   14.58

Step 5:   Add: Dividends earned since the buy signal
10.32 × 5.91% × (281 ÷ 365) =   0.47

Step 6:   Total value of the WSTL's investment in the S&P 500   15.05

Step 7:   WSTL's annual return
Total value from step 6 ÷ S&P 500 closing price at the end of 1937
(15.05 ÷ 10.55) − 1.00 =   42.65%

Exhibit D-4: Panel 2 (continued)

1942

Step 1:   Total value of the WSTL's investment in the S&P 500 at the sell signal, 3/06/42
S&P 500 closing price + year-to-date dividend earned
8.16 + (8.69 × 7.91%) × (65 ÷ 365) =   8.28

Step 2:   The buy signal was triggered by the lower limit on 4/17/42.
Add: Interest earned while WSTL was red (measured in terms of the WSTL's
investment in the S&P 500 at the sell signal)
8.28 × 0.28% × (42 ÷ 365) =   0.00

Step 3:   Total value of the WSTL's investment in 3-month T-bills (measured in terms of
the S&P 500 closing price on the day of the buy signal)   8.28

Year-end 1942

Step 4:   Total value of the WSTL's investment in the S&P 500 at year-end (not including
dividends earned since the buy signal)
Total value from step 3 × Percentage change in S&P 500 since the buy signal
8.28 × (9.77 ÷ 7.70) =   10.51

Step 5:   Add: Dividends earned since the buy signal
8.28 × 7.91% × (258 ÷ 365) =   0.46

Step 6:   Total value of the WSTL's investment in the S&P 500   10.97

Step 7:   WSTL annual return
Total value from step 6 ÷ S&P 500 closing price at the end of 1941
(10.97 ÷ 8.69) − 1.00 =   26.24%

1946

Step 1:   Total value of the WSTL's investment in the S&P 500 at the sell signal, 2/25/46
S&P 500 closing price + year-to-date dividend earned
16.91 + (17.36 × 3.80%) × (56 ÷ 365) =   17.01

Step 2:   The buy signal was triggered by the lower limit on 9/03/46.
Add: Interest earned while WSTL was red (measured in terms of the WSTL's
investment in the S&P 500 at the sell signal)
17.01 × 0.38% × (190 ÷ 365) =   0.03

Step 3:   Total value of the WSTL's investment in 3-month T-bills (measured in terms of
the S&P 500 closing price on the day of the buy signal)   17.04

Year-end 1946

Step 4:   Total value of the WSTL's investment in the S&P 500 at year-end (not including
dividends earned since the buy signal)
Total value from step 3 × Percentage change in S&P 500 since the buy signal
17.04 × (15.30 ÷ 15.00) =   17.38

Step 5:   Add: Dividends earned since the buy signal
17.04 × 3.80% × (119 ÷ 365) =   0.21

Step 6:   Total value of the WSTL's investment in the S&P 500   17.59

Step 7:   WSTL annual return
Total value from step 6 ÷ S&P 500 closing price at the end of 1945
(17.59 ÷ 17.36) − 1.00 =   1.32%

Exhibit D-4: Panel 2 continues on the next page.

Exhibit D-4: Panel 2 (continued)

1947

Step 1: Total value of the WSTL's investment in the S&P 500 at the sell signal, 4/14/47
S&P 500 closing price + year-to-date dividend earned
$14.14 + (15.30 \times 5.71\%) \times (104 \div 365) =$ — 14.39

Step 2: The buy signal was triggered by the lower limit on 5/17/47.
Add: Interest earned while WSTL was red (measured in terms of the WSTL's investment in the S&P 500 at the sell signal)
$14.39 \times 0.38\% \times (33 \div 365) =$ — 0.00

Step 3: Total value of the WSTL's investment in 3-month T-bills (measured in terms of the S&P 500 closing price on the day of the buy signal) — 14.39

Year-end 1947

Step 4: Total value of the WSTL's investment in the S&P 500 at year-end (not including dividends earned since the buy signal)
Total value from step 3 × Percentage change in S&P 500 since the buy signal
$14.39 \times (15.30 \div 13.71) =$ — 16.06

Step 5: Add: Dividends earned since the buy signal
$14.39 \times 5.71\% \times (228 \div 365) =$ — 0.51

Step 6: Total value of the WSTL's investment in the S&P 500 — 16.57

Step 7: WSTL annual return
Total value from step 6 ÷ S&P 500 closing price at the end of 1946
$(16.57 \div 15.30) - 1.00 =$ — **8.30%**

1949

Step 1: Total value of the WSTL's investment in the S&P 500 at the sell signal, 2/05/49
S&P 500 closing price + year-to-date dividend earned
$14.85 + (15.20 \times 8.53\%) \times (36 \div 365) =$ — 14.98

Step 2: The buy signal was triggered by the lower limit on 6/13/49.
Add: Interest earned while WSTL was red (measured in terms of the WSTL's investment in the S&P 500 at the sell signal)
$14.98 \times 1.17\% \times (128 \div 365) =$ — 0.06

Step 3: Total value of the WSTL's investment in 3-month T-bills (measured in terms of the S&P 500 closing price on the day of the buy signal) — 15.04

Year-end 1949

Step 4: Total value of the WSTL's investment in the S&P 500 at year-end (not including dividends earned since the buy signal)
Total value from step 3 × Percentage change in S&P 500 since the buy signal
$15.04 \times (16.76 \div 13.55) =$ — 18.60

Step 5: Add: Dividends earned since the buy signal
$15.04 \times 8.53\% \times (201 \div 365) =$ — 0.71

Step 6: Total value of the WSTL's investment in the S&P 500 — 19.31

Step 7: WSTL annual return
Total value from step 6 ÷ S&P 500 closing price at the end of 1948
$(19.31 \div 15.20) - 1.00 =$ — **27.04%**

Exhibit D-4: Panel 2 (continued)

1966

Step 1: Total value of the WSTL's investment in the S&P 500 at the sell signal, 3/01/66
S&P 500 closing price + year-to-date dividend earned
90.06 + (92.43 × 3.03%) × (60 ÷ 365) =   90.52

Step 2: The buy signal was triggered by the lower limit on 8/01/66.
Add: Interest earned while WSTL was red (measured in terms of the WSTL's
investment in the S&P 500 at the sell signal)
90.52 × 4.63% × (153 ÷ 365) =   1.76

Step 3: Total value of the WSTL's investment in 3-month T-bills (measured in terms of
the S&P 500 closing price on the day of the buy signal)   92.28

Year-end 1966

Step 4: Total value of the WSTL's investment in the S&P 500 at year-end (not including
dividends earned since the buy signal)
Total value from step 3 × Percentage change in S&P 500 since the buy signal
92.28 × (80.33 ÷ 82.31) =   90.06

Step 5: Add: Dividends earned since the buy signal
92.28 × 3.03% × (152 ÷ 365) =   1.16

Step 6: Total value of the WSTL's investment in the S&P 500   91.22

Step 7: WSTL annual return
Total value from step 6 ÷ S&P 500 closing price at the end of 1965
(91.22 ÷ 92.43) − 1.00 =   −1.31%

Exhibit D-5

Details of WSTL Trades and Returns for Category "C" Years, 1935-1969

Panel 1: Basic Data for Trades in Category "C" Years

Year	Sell Signal	Buy Signal	S&P 500 Closing Price				S&P 500 Annual Dividend Yield*	Average Annual Rate on 3-mo. T-Bills#	Three Segments of Year (calendar days)		
			End of Prior Year	Sell Signal	Buy Signal	End of Year			Start of Year to Sell Signal (Green Light)	Sell Signal to Buy Signal (Red Light)	Buy Signal to Year-End (Green Light)
1935	End 1/35	03/14/35	9.50	9.10	8.06	13.43	6.30%	0.17%	31	42	292
1939	End 1/39	04/06/39	13.21	12.30	10.66	12.49	5.04%	0.03%	31	65	269
1940	End 1/40	05/14/40	12.49	12.05	10.28	10.58	5.51%	0.03%	31	104	231
1941	End 1/41	End 11/41	10.58	10.07	9.10	8.69	6.27%	0.12%	31	303	31
1948	End 1/48	End 11/48	15.30	14.69	14.75	15.20	6.16%	1.04%	31	304	31
1953	02/17/53	09/14/53	26.57	25.50	22.71	24.81	5.63%	2.04%	48	209	108
1956	End 1/56	End 11/56	45.48	43.82	45.08	46.67	3.94%	2.59%	31	304	31
1957	End 1/57	10/21/57	46.67	44.72	39.15	39.99	3.53%	3.25%	31	246	88
1960	End 1/60	End 11/60	59.89	55.61	55.54	58.11	3.45%	2.80%	31	304	31
1962	End 1/62	05/23/62	71.55	68.84	61.11	63.10	3.08%	2.72%	31	112	222
1968	End 1/68	11/26/68	96.47	92.24	107.26	103.86	3.40%	5.31%	31	300	35
1969	End 1/69	07/28/69	103.86	103.01	90.21	92.06	2.86%	6.29%	31	178	156

*assumed to be evenly distributed during the year.

#while the WSTL was red.

Exhibit D-5, Panel 2: Calculating the WSTL Returns for Category "C" Years

1935

Step 1: Total value of the WSTL investment in the S&P 500 at the sell signal, end 1/35 S&P 500 closing price + year-to-date dividend earned
9.10 + (9.50 × 6.30%) × (31 ÷ 365) =   9.15

Step 2: The buy signal was triggered by the lower limit on 3/14/35.
Add: Interest earned while WSTL was red (measured in terms of the WSTL's investment in the S&P 500 at the sell signal)
9.15 × 0.17% × (42 ÷ 365) =   0.00

Step 3: Total value of the WSTL investment in 3-month T-bills (measured in terms of the S&P 500 closing price on the day of the buy signal)   9.15

Year-end 1935

Step 4: Total value of the WSTL investment in the S&P 500 at year-end (not including dividends earned since the buy signal)
Total value from step 3 × Percentage change in S&P 500 since the buy signal
9.15 × (13.43 ÷ 8.06) =   15.25

Step 5: Add: Dividends earned since the buy signal
9.15 × 6.30% × (292 ÷ 365) =   0.46

Step 6: Total value of the WSTL investment in the S&P 500   15.71

Step 7: WSTL annual return
Total value from step 6 ÷ S&P 500 closing price at the end of 1934
(15.71 ÷ 9.50) − 1.00 =   65.37%

1939

Step 1: Total value of the WSTL investment in the S&P 500 at the sell signal, end 1/39 S&P 500 closing price + year-to-date dividend earned
12.30 + (13.21 × 5.04%) × (31 ÷ 365) =   12.36

Step 2: The buy signal was triggered by the lower limit on 4/06/39.
Add: Interest earned while WSTL was red (measured in terms of the WSTL's investment in the S&P 500 at the sell signal)
12.36 × 0.03% × (65 ÷ 365) =   0.00

Step 3: Total value of the WSTL investment in 3-month T-bills (measured in terms of the S&P 500 closing price on the day of the buy signal)   12.36

Year-end 1939

Step 4: Total value of the WSTL investment in the S&P 500 at year-end (not including dividends earned since the buy signal)
Total value from step 3 × Percentage change in S&P 500 since the buy signal
12.36 × (12.49 ÷ 10.66) =   14.48

Step 5: Add: Dividends earned since the buy signal
12.36 × 5.04% × (269 ÷ 365) =   0.46

Step 6: Total value of the WSTL investment in the S&P 500   14.94

Step 7: WSTL annual return
Total value from step 6 ÷ S&P 500 closing price at the end of 1938
(14.94 ÷ 13.21) − 1.00 =   13.10%

Exhibit D-5: Panel 2 continues on the next page.

Exhibit D-5: Panel 2 (continued)

1940

Step 1: Total value of the WSTL investment in the S&P 500 at the sell signal, end 1/40
S&P 500 closing price + year-to-date dividend earned
$12.05 + (12.49 \times 5.51\%) \times (31 \div 366) =$ 12.11

Step 2: The buy signal was triggered by the lower limit on 5/14/40.
Add: Interest earned while WSTL was red (measured in terms of the WSTL's
investment in the S&P 500 at the sell signal)
$12.11 \times 0.03\% \times (104 \div 366) =$ 0.00

Step 3: Total value of the WSTL investment in 3-month T-bills (measured in terms of the
S&P 500 closing price on the day of the buy signal)   12.11

Year-end 1940

Step 4: Total value of the WSTL investment in the S&P 500 at year-end (not including
dividends earned since the buy signal)
Total value from step 3 × Percentage change in S&P 500 since the buy signal
$12.11 \times (10.58 \div 10.28) =$ 12.46

Step 5: Add: Dividends earned since the buy signal
$12.11 \times 5.51\% \times (231 \div 366) =$ 0.42

Step 6: Total value of the WSTL investment in the S&P 500   12.88

Step 7: WSTL annual return
Total value from step 6 ÷ S&P 500 closing price at the end of 1939
$(12.88 \div 12.49) - 1.00 =$ 3.12%

1941

Step 1: Total value of the WSTL investment in the S&P 500 at the sell signal, end 1/41 S&P
500 closing price + year-to-date dividend earned
$10.07 + (10.58 \times 6.27\%) \times (31 \div 365) =$ 10.13

Step 2: The buy signal was triggered by the time limit at the end 11/41.
Add: Interest earned while WSTL was red (measured in terms of the WSTL's
investment in the S&P 500 at the sell signal)
$10.13 \times 0.12\% \times (303 \div 365) =$ 0.01

Step 3: Total value of the WSTL investment in 3-month T-bills (measured in terms of the
S&P 500 closing price on the day of the buy signal)   10.14

Year-end 1941

Step 4: Total value of the WSTL investment in the S&P 500 at year-end (not including
dividends earned since the buy signal)
Total value from step 3 × Percentage change in S&P 500 since the buy signal
$10.14 \times (8.69 \div 9.10) =$ 9.68

Step 5: Add: Dividends earned since the buy signal
$10.14 \times 6.27\% \times (31 \div 365) =$ 0.05

Step 6: Total value of the WSTL investment in the S&P 500   9.73

Step 7: WSTL annual return
Total value from step 6 ÷ S&P 500 closing price at the end of 1940
$(9.73 \div 10.58) - 1.00 =$ −8.03%

Exhibit D-5: Panel 2 (continued)

1948

Step 1: Total value of the WSTL investment in the S&P 500 at the sell signal, end 1/48 S&P 500 closing price + year-to-date dividend earned
$$14.69 + (15.30 \times 6.16\%) \times (31 \div 366) =$$ 14.77

Step 2: The buy signal was triggered by the time limit at the end 11/48.
Add: Interest earned while WSTL was red (measured in terms of the WSTL's investment in the S&P 500 at the sell signal)
$$14.77 \times 1.04\% \times (304 \div 366) =$$ 0.13

Step 3: Total value of the WSTL investment in 3-month T-bills (measured in terms of the S&P 500 closing price on the day of the buy signal) 14.90

Year-end 1948

Step 4: Total value of the WSTL investment in the S&P 500 at year-end (not including dividends earned since the buy signal)
Total value from step 3 × Percentage change in S&P 500 since the buy signal
$$14.90 \times (15.20 \div 14.75) =$$ 15.35

Step 5: Add: Dividends earned since the buy signal
$$14.90 \times 6.16\% \times (31 \div 366) =$$ 0.08

Step 6: Total value of the WSTL investment in the S&P 500 15.43

Step 7: WSTL annual return
Total value from step 6 ÷ S&P 500 closing price at the end of 1947
$$(15.43 \div 15.30) - 1.00 =$$ 0.85%

1953

Step 1: Total value of the WSTL investment in the S&P 500 at the sell signal, 2/17/53 S&P 500 closing price + year-to-date dividend earned
$$25.50 + (26.57 \times 5.63\%) \times (48 \div 365) =$$ 25.70

Step 2: The buy signal was triggered by the lower limit on 9/14/53.
Add: Interest earned while WSTL was red (measured in terms of the WSTL's investment in the S&P 500 at the sell signal)
$$25.70 \times 2.04\% \times (209 \div 365) =$$ 0.30

Step 3: Total value of the WSTL investment in 3-month T-bills (measured in terms of the S&P 500 closing price on the day of the buy signal) 26.00

Year-end 1953

Step 4: Total value of the WSTL investment in the S&P 500 at year-end (not including dividends earned since the buy signal)
Total value from step 3 × Percentage change in S&P 500 since the buy signal
$$26.00 \times (24.81 \div 22.71) =$$ 28.40

Step 5: Add: Dividends earned since the buy signal
$$26.00 \times 5.63\% \times (108 \div 365) =$$ 0.43

Step 6: Total value of the WSTL investment in the S&P 500 28.83

Step 7: WSTL annual return
Total value from step 6 ÷ S&P 500 closing price at the end of 1952
$$(28.83 \div 26.57) - 1.00 =$$ 8.51%

Exhibit D-5: Panel 2 continues on the next page.

Exhibit D-5: Panel 2 (continued)

1956

Step 1: Total value of the WSTL investment in the S&P 500 at the sell signal, end 1/56
S&P 500 closing price + year-to-date dividend earned
$$43.82 + (45.48 \times 3.94\%) \times (31 \div 366) =$$ 43.97

Step 2: The buy signal was triggered by the time limit at the end 11/56.
Add: Interest earned while WSTL was red (measured in terms of the WSTL's
investment in the S&P 500 at the sell signal)
$$43.97 \times 2.59\% \times (304 \div 366) =$$ 0.95

Step 3: Total value of the WSTL investment in 3-month T-bills (measured in terms of the
S&P 500 closing price on the day of the buy signal) 44.92

Year-end 1956

Step 4: Total value of the WSTL investment in the S&P 500 at year-end (not including
dividends earned since the buy signal)
Total value from step 3 × Percentage change in S&P 500 since the buy signal
$$44.92 \times (46.67 \div 45.08) =$$ 46.50

Step 5: Add: Dividends earned since the buy signal
$$44.92 \times 3.94\% \times (31 \div 366) =$$ 0.15

Step 6: Total value of the WSTL investment in the S&P 500 46.65

Step 7: WSTL annual return
Total value from step 6 ÷ S&P 500 closing price at the end of 1955
$$(46.65 \div 45.48) - 1.00 =$$ 2.57%

1957

Step 1: Total value of the WSTL investment in the S&P 500 at the sell signal, end 1/57 S&P
500 closing price + year-to-date dividend earned
$$44.72 + (46.67 \times 3.53\%) \times (31 \div 365) =$$ 44.86

Step 2: The buy signal was triggered by the lower limit on 10/21/57.
Add: Interest earned while WSTL was red (measured in terms of the WSTL's
investment in the S&P 500 at the sell signal)
$$44.86 \times 3.25\% \times (246 \div 365) =$$ 0.98

Step 3: Total value of the WSTL investment in 3-month T-bills (measured in terms of the
S&P 500 closing price on the day of the buy signal) 45.84

Year-end 1957

Step 4: Total value of the WSTL investment in the S&P 500 at year-end (not including
dividends earned since the buy signal)
Total value from step 3 × Percentage change in S&P 500 since the buy signal
$$45.84 \times (39.99 \div 39.15) =$$ 46.82

Step 5: Add: Dividends earned since the buy signal
$$45.84 \times 3.53\% \times (88 \div 365) =$$ 0.39

Step 6: Total value of the WSTL investment in the S&P 500 47.21

Step 7: WSTL annual return
Total value from step 6 ÷ S&P 500 closing price at the end of 1956
$$(47.21 \div 46.67) - 1.00 =$$ 1.16%

Exhibit D-5: Panel 2 (continued)

1960

Step 1:   Total value of the WSTL investment in the S&P 500 at the sell signal, end 1/60 S&P
          500 closing price + year-to-date dividend earned
          $55.61 + (59.89 \times 3.45\%) \times (31 \div 366) =$ 55.79

Step 2:   The buy signal was triggered by the time limit at the end 11/60.
          Add: Interest earned while WSTL was red (measured in terms of the WSTL's
          investment in the S&P 500 at the sell signal)
          $55.79 \times 2.80\% \times (304 \div 366) =$ 1.30

Step 3:   Total value of the WSTL investment in 3-month T-bills (measured in terms of
          the S&P 500 closing price on the day of the buy signal)   57.09

          Year-end 1960

Step 4:   Total value of the WSTL investment in the S&P 500 at year-end (not including
          dividends earned since the buy signal)
          Total value from step 3 × Percentage change in S&P 500 since the buy signal
          $57.09 \times (58.11 \div 55.54) =$ 59.73

Step 5:   Add: Dividends earned since the buy signal
          $57.09 \times 3.45\% \times (31 \div 366) =$ 0.17

Step 6:   Total value of the WSTL investment in the S&P 500   59.90

Step 7:   WSTL annual return
          Total value from step 6 ÷ S&P 500 closing price at the end of 1959
          $(59.90 \div 59.89) - 1.00 =$ 0.02%

1962

Step 1:   Total value of the WSTL investment in the S&P 500 at the sell signal, end 1/62 S&P
          500 closing price + year-to-date dividend earned
          $68.84 + (71.55 \times 3.08\%) \times (31 \div 365) =$ 69.03

Step 2:   The buy signal was triggered by the lower limit on 5/23/62.
          Add: Interest earned while WSTL was red (measured in terms of the WSTL's
          investment in the S&P 500 at the sell signal)
          $69.03 \times 2.72\% \times (112 \div 365) =$ 0.58

Step 3:   Total value of the WSTL investment in 3-month T-bills (measured in terms of
          the S&P 500 closing price on the day of the buy signal)   69.61

          Year-end 1962

Step 4:   Total value of the WSTL investment in the S&P 500 at year-end (not including
          dividends earned since the buy signal)
          Total value from step 3 × Percentage change in S&P 500 since the buy signal
          $69.61 \times (63.10 \div 61.11) =$ 71.88

Step 5:   Add: Dividends earned since the buy signal
          $69.61 \times 3.08\% \times (222 \div 365) =$ 1.30

Step 6:   Total value of the WSTL investment in the S&P 500   73.18

Step 7:   WSTL annual return
          Total value from step 6 ÷ S&P 500 closing price at the end of 1961
          $(73.18 \div 71.55) - 1.00 =$ 2.28%

Exhibit D-5: Panel 2 continues on the next page.

Exhibit D-5: Panel 2 (continued)

1968

Step 1: Total value of the WSTL investment in the S&P 500 at the sell signal, end 1/68 S&P
500 closing price + year-to-date dividend earned
$92.24 + (96.47 \times 3.40\%) \times (31 \div 366) =$ 92.52

Step 2: The buy signal was triggered by the upper limit on 11/26/68.
Add: Interest earned while WSTL was red (measured in terms of the WSTL's
investment in the S&P 500 at the sell signal)
$92.52 \times 5.31\% \times (300 \div 366) =$ 4.03

Step 3: Total value of the WSTL investment in 3-month T-bills (measured in terms of
the S&P 500 closing price on the day of buy signal)   96.55

Year-end 1968

Step 4: Total value of the WSTL investment in the S&P 500 at year-end (not including
dividends earned since the buy signal)
Total value from step 3 × Percentage change in S&P 500 since the buy signal
$96.55 \times (103.86 \div 107.26) =$ 93.49

Step 5: Add: Dividends earned since the buy signal
$96.55 \times 3.40\% \times (35 \div 366) =$ 0.31

Step 6: Total value of the WSTL investment in the S&P 500   93.80

Step 7: WSTL annual return
Total value from step 6 ÷ S&P 500 closing price at the end of 1967
$(93.80 \div 96.47) - 1.00 =$ −2.77%

1969

Step 1: Total value of the WSTL investment in the S&P 500 at the sell signal, end 1/69 S&P
500 closing price + year-to-date dividend earned
$103.01 + (103.86 \times 2.86\%) \times (31 \div 365) =$ 103.26

Step 2: The buy signal was triggered by the lower limit on 7/28/69.
Add: Interest earned while WSTL was red (measured in terms of the WSTL's
investment in the S&P 500 at the sell signal)
$103.26 \times 6.29\% \times (178 \div 365) =$ 3.17

Step 3: Total value of the WSTL investment in 3-month T-bills (measured in terms of the
S&P 500 closing price on the day of the buy signal)   106.43

Year-end 1969

Step 4: Total value of the WSTL investment in the S&P 500 at year-end (not including
dividends earned since the buy signal)
Total value from step 3 × Percentage change in S&P 500 since the buy signal
$106.43 \times (92.06 \div 90.21) =$ 108.61

Step 5: Add: Dividends earned since the buy signal
$106.43 \times 2.86\% \times (156 \div 365) =$ 1.30

Step 6: Total value of the WSTL investment in the S&P 500   109.91

Step 7: WSTL annual return
Total value from step 6 ÷ S&P 500 closing price at the end of 1968
$(109.91 \div 103.86) - 1.00 =$ 5.83%

Appendix E

◇◇◇◇◇◇◇◇◇◇◇◇◇

ANNUAL RETURNS, CAGR AND RISK, 1935-1969

This appendix presents the return and risk statistics for the WSTL strategy for the sample period and compares that performance to the strategy of buying-and-holding the S&P 500. The material here is in the same sequence as the return and risk statistics for 1970-2006 presented in Chapters 3 and 4.

Returns for 1A, 3A and Tier 2 Years

Of the 35 years comprising 1935-1969, eight were 1A years and three were 3A years. Exhibit E-1 presents the returns for those years, ranked from best to worst. The mean of those years was 25.6%, which is 12 percentage points above the mean return of 13.6% for all years during 1935-1969.

Exhibit E-1

Returns for the 1A and 3A Years, 1935-1969

For these years, the WSTL return is the same as the S&P 500 return.

Year	Type of Year	Return (ranked best to worst)
1958	3A	43.4%
1945	1A	36.4%
1936	1A	33.9%
1955	1A	31.6%
1943	3A	25.9%
1951	1A	24.0%
1967	3A	24.0%
1944	1A	19.8%
1952	1A	18.4%
1965	1A	12.5%
1959	1A	12.0%
Mean		25.6%

There were six Tier 2 years during 1935-1969. Exhibit E-2 presents the returns for those years, ranked from best to worst. The mean return of those years was 26.9%, which was almost double the mean return for all years during 1935-1969.

Exhibit E-2

Returns for the Tier 2 Years, 1935-1969

For these years, the WSTL return is the same as the S&P 500 return.

Year	Return (ranked best to worst)
1954	52.6%
1950	31.7%
1961	26.9%
1963	22.8%
1964	16.5%
1968	11.1%
Mean	26.9%

Returns and Total Accumulations for 1935-1969

Exhibit E-3 presents the annual returns for the WSTL and buying-and-holding the S&P 500 for 1935-1969. The returns for the 1A, 3A and Tier 2 years are from the first two exhibits in this appendix. The returns for the 1B, 1C, 3B and 3C years are from Exhibit 9-3 (p. 82).

To calculate the total accumulations for 1935-1969, Exhibit E-3 is based on the following assumptions: (i) 401(k)s and IRAs existed throughout the period, (ii) dividends and interest were reinvested and (iii) there were no investment costs. That set of assumptions makes Exhibit E-3 comparable to Exhibit 3-3 (p. XX), which is for 1970-2006. The shaded total-accumulation figures near the bottom of Exhibit E-3 indicate that the WSTL grew $10,000 to $1,776,418, while buy-and-hold grew $10,000 to $502,679. That is, the WSTL's total accumulation was 253% greater than buy-and-hold [($1,776,418 − $502,679) ÷ $502,679 = 253%].

The compound annual growth rates (CAGRs) are the shaded percentages on the bottom row of Exhibit E-3: 15.95% for the WSTL and 11.84% for buy-and-hold—a difference of 4.11 percentage points.

Exhibit E-3

Annual Returns and Total Accumulations for 1935-1969

Year	Type of Year	WSTL Return	End-of-Year Accumulation from One-Time Investment of $10,000 Using the WSTL	S&P 500 Return	End-of-Year Accumulation from One-Time Investment of $10,000 in the S&P 500
1934			$10,000		$10,000
1935	1C	65.4%	$16,540	47.7%	$14,770
1936	1A	33.9%	$22,147	33.9%	$19,777
1937	1B	−32.0%	$15,060	−35.0%	$12,855
1938	3B	42.7%	$21,491	31.1%	$16,853
1939	3C	13.1%	$24,306	−0.4%	$16,786
1940	1C	3.1%	$25,059	−9.8%	$15,141
1941	3C	−8.0%	$23,055	−11.6%	$13,384
1942	3B	26.2%	$29,095	20.3%	$16,101
1943	3A	25.9%	$36,631	25.9%	$20,272
1944	1A	19.8%	$43,883	19.8%	$24,285
1945	1A	36.4%	$59,857	36.4%	$33,125
1946	1B	1.3%	$60,635	−8.1%	$30,442
1947	1B	8.3%	$65,668	5.7%	$32,177
1948	3C	0.9%	$66,259	5.5%	$33,947
1949	3B	7.0%	$84,149	18.8%	$40,329
1950	Tier 2	31.7%	$110,824	31.7%	$53,118
1951	1A	24.0%	$137,421	24.0%	$65,866
1952	1A	18.4%	$162,707	18.4%	$77,985
1953	1C	8.5%	$176,537	−1.0%	$77,205
1954	Tier 2	52.6%	$269,396	52.6%	$117,833
1955	1A	31.6%	$354,525	31.6%	$155,068
1956	1C	2.6%	$363,742	6.6%	$165,303
1957	1C	1.2%	$368,107	−10.8%	$147,450
1958	3A	43.4%	$527,866	43.4%	$211,443
1959	1A	12.0%	$591,210	12.0%	$236,817
1960	1C	0.0%	$591,210	0.5%	$238,001
1961	Tier 2	26.9%	$750,245	26.9%	$302,023
1962	1C	2.3%	$767,501	−8.7%	$275,747
1963	Tier 2	22.8%	$942,491	22.8%	$338,618

Exhibit E-3 continues on the next page.

Exhibit E-3 (continued)

Year	Type of Year	WSTL Return	End-of-Year Accumulation from One-Time Investment of $10,000 Using the WSTL	S&P 500 Return	End-of-Year Accumulation from One-Time Investment of $10,000 in the S&P 500
1964	Tier 2	16.5%	$1,098,002	16.5%	$394,431
1965	1A	12.5%	$1,235,252	12.5%	$443,734
1966	1B	−1.3%	$1,219,194	−10.1%	$398,917
1967	3A	24.0%	$1,511,800	24.0%	$494,657
1968	Tier 2	11.1%	$1,679,034	11.1%	$549,376
1969	1C	5.8%	$1,776,418	−8.5%	$502,679
CAGR		15.95%		11.84%	

Risk Profiles for 1935-1969

This section presents the same eight measures of risk discussed in Chapter 4 for 1970-2006. Each measure indicates that, for 1935-1969, the WSTL had lower risk compared to buying-and-holding the S&P 500.

1. **Variability of Annual Returns.** For 1935-1969, the WSTL strategy had a standard deviation of 18.7% compared to 19.7% for buy-and-hold. Since the WSTL's standard deviation was 1.0 percentage point less, that represents 5.1% lower risk: −1.0 ÷ 19.7 = −5.1%.

2. **Depth and Duration of Downside Volatility.** This measure of risk is called the ulcer index. For 1935-2006, the ulcer index for the WSTL strategy was 11.2% and for buy-and-hold was 22.9%. The WSTL's ulcer index being 11.7 percentage points less represents 51.1% lower risk: −11.7 ÷ 22.9 = −51.1%. The detailed calculations that yielded these ulcer indexes are available at thewallstreettrafficlight.com.

3. **Maximum Number of Years Needed to Avoid a Loss.** To determine this measure of risk, look at the "End-of-Year Accumulation" columns in Exhibit E-3. For the WSTL, the maximum number of years needed to avoid a loss was three—which was the 1937-1939 period. The total accumulation at the end of 1936 was $22,147, which was not exceeded until the end of 1939. For buy-and-hold, the maximum number of years needed to avoid a loss was seven—which was the 1937-1943 period. The total accumulation at the end of 1936 was $19,777, which was not exceeded until the end of 1943. Since the WSTL's maximum period was four years shorter, that represents 57.1% lower risk: −4 ÷ 7 = −57.1%.

4. **Negative Annual Returns.** The simplest way to use negative annual returns to gauge risk for 1935-1969 is to compare the WSTL's worst year (it was 1937, which had a return of −32.0%) to the S&P 500's worst year (it also was 1937, which had

a return of −35.0%). Although the WSTL's return for 1937 was negative, it was 3.0 percentage points better than the S&P 500's return for that year, representing 8.6% lower risk: 3.0 ÷ −35.0 = −8.6%.

The following table (derived from Exhibit E-3) provides three more ways to measure risk using the negative annual returns during 1935-1969:

Negative Annual Returns	WSTL	S&P 500	WSTL Advantage	Extent of WSTL's Lower Risk
◆ Number of years	3	10	7 years	−7 ÷ 10 = −70.0%
◆ Mean annual return for WSTL's three years having negative returns	−13.8%	−18.9%	5.1 percentage points	5.1 ÷ −18.9 = −27.0%
◆ Mean annual return for the S&P 500's ten years having negative returns	−0.6%	−10.4%	9.8 percentage points	9.8 ÷ −10.4 = −94.2%

All three measures indicate that the WSTL strategy had lower risk.

Exhibit E-4 provides the supporting details for the last item in the table. In each of the ten years when the S&P 500 had a negative return, there was a profitable trade.

Exhibit E-4

WSTL Returns for Years When the S&P 500 Returns Were Negative, 1935-1969

Year	Type of Year	WSTL Return	S&P 500 Return	Outcome Of Trade
1937	1B	−32.0%	−35.0%	3.0%
1939	3C	13.1%	−0.4%	13.5%
1940	1C	3.1%	−9.8%	12.9%
1941	3C	−8.0%	−11.6%	3.6%
1946	1B	1.3%	−8.1%	9.4%
1953	1C	8.5%	−1.0%	9.5%
1957	1C	1.2%	−10.8%	11.9%*
1962	1C	2.3%	−8.7%	11.0%*
1966	1B	−1.3%	−10.1%	8.8%
1969	1C	5.8%	−8.5%	14.3%
Mean		−0.6%	−10.4%	9.8%

*This difference does not add across due to rounding.

5. **Maximum Year-to-Date Declines of 10% or More.** For 1935-1969, 16 of the 35 years had a maximum year-to-date decline of 10% or more in the S&P 500. Exhibit E-5 lists those declines and the accompanying maximum year-to-date declines under the WSTL strategy. The mean of the columns' declines were 19.2% and 11.0%, respectively. Since the WSTL strategy's mean maximum year-to-date decline was 8.2 percentage points less, that represents 42.7% lower risk: $-8.2 \div 19.2 = -42.7\%$. That lower risk was due to the fact that there was a profitable trade in all but one of the years in the exhibit; the trade in 1960 lost 0.5%.

Exhibit E-5

WSTL Maximum Year-to-Date Declines During Years When the S&P 500 Maximum Year-to-Date Declines Were 10% or More, 1935-1969

Year	S&P 500 Maximum Year-to-Date Decline	Type of Year	WSTL Maximum Year-to-Date Decline	Outcome of Trade
1935	15.2%	1C	4.2%	17.7%
1937	40.8%	1B	37.1%	3.0%
1938	19.4%	3B	12.2%	11.5%
1939	22.9%	3C	11.1%	13.5%
1940	28.0%	1C	15.6%	12.9%
1941	20.9%	3C	12.5%	3.6%
1942	14.0%	3B	9.8%	5.9%
1946	18.7%	1B	8.3%	9.4%
1947	10.4%	1B	7.6%	2.6%
1949	10.9%	3B	3.3%	8.3%
1953	14.5%	1C	4.0%	9.5%
1957	16.5%	1C	4.6%	11.9%
1960	12.7%	1C	12.6%	−0.5%
1962	26.9%	1C	17.6%	11.0%
1966	20.8%	1B	13.3%	8.8%
1969	14.1%	1C	1.9%	14.3%
Mean	19.2%		11.0%	8.2%

Summary

Exhibit E-6, which is identical to Exhibit 5-2 (42), summarizes the return and risk statistics presented in this appendix.

Exhibit E-6

Performance Summary for 1935-1969

Performance Measure	WSTL (18 round-trip trades)	Buy-and-Hold S&P 500	WSTL Advantage	WSTL Percentage Advantage
Returns				
Total accumulation from a one-time investment of $10,000 at the end of 1934 (re-investing dividends and interest, ignoring investment costs and income taxes)	$1,776,418	$502,679	$1,273,739	253%
Compound annual growth rate (CAGR)	15.95%	11.84%	4.11 % points	34.7%
Risk				
Variability of annual returns (standard deviation)	18.7%	19.7%	1.0 % points	5.1%
Depth and duration of downside volatility (ulcer index)	11.2%	22.9%	11.7 % points	51.1%
Maximum number of years needed to avoid a loss	3 years	7 years	4 years	57.1%
Worst year (It was 1937 under both strategies.)	−32.0%	−35.0%	3.0 % points	8.6%
Negative annual returns				
◆ Number of times	3 years	10 years	7 years	70.0%
◆ Mean annual return for WSTL's five years having negative returns	−13.8%	−18.9%	5.1 % points	27.0%
◆ Mean annual return for S&P 500's eight years having negative returns	−0.6%	−10.4%	9.8 % points	94.2%
Maximum year-to-date declines of 10% or more (mean for the 16 cases)	11.0%	19.2%	8.2 % points	42.7%

Appendix F

◇◇◇◇◇◇◇◇◇◇◇◇◇◇

CALCULATING THE RETURNS FOR YEARS
WITH TRADES, 1970-2006

This appendix consists of two exhibits. Exhibit F-1 summarizes the 13 trades during 1970-2006. Exhibit F-2 provides the details of the trades and calculates the WSTL return for each of those years.

Exhibit F-1

Trades During 1970-2006

Year	Type of Year	Trigger for Buy Signal	WSTL Return	S&P 500 Return	Outcome of Trade
1970	3C	Lower limit	17.7%	4.0%	13.7%
1973	1C	Lower limit	−3.0%	−14.7%	11.7%
1974	3C	Lower limit	−16.0%	−26.5%	10.5%
1977	1C	Lower limit	4.5%	−7.2%	11.7%
1981	1C	Lower limit	13.1%	−4.9%	18.0%
1982	1C	Lower limit	39.8%	21.4%	18.4%
1984	1C	Time limit	8.7%	6.3%	2.4%
1990	1C	Time limit	2.1%	−3.2%	5.2%*
2000	1C	Time limit	0.1%	−9.1%	9.2%
2001	3B	Lower limit	−6.3%	−11.9%	5.6%
2002	3C	Lower limit	−12.6%	−22.1%	9.5%
2003	3C	Upper limit	10.3%	28.7%	−18.4%
2005	1C	Time limit	−0.2%	4.9%	−5.1%
Mean			4.5%	−2.6%	7.1%

*This difference does not add across due to rounding.

141

Exhibit F-2

Details of WSTL Trades and Returns for Those Years, 1970-2006

Panel 1: Basic Data for Trades

Year	Sell Signal	Buy Signal	S&P 500 Closing Price				S&P 500 Annual Dividend Yield*	Average Annual Rate on 3-mo. T-Bills#	Three Segments of Year (calendar days)		
			End of Prior Year	Sell Signal	Buy Signal	End of Year			Start of Year to Sell Signal (Green Light)	Sell Signal to Buy Signal (Red Light)	Buy Signal to Year-End (Green Light)
1970	End 1/70	05/14/70	92.06	85.02	75.44	92.15	3.91%	6.78%	31	103	231
1973	02/01/73	07/03/73	118.05	114.76	101.87	97.55	2.70%	6.08%	32	152	181
1974	02/11/74	07/10/74	97.55	90.66	79.99	68.56	3.25%	7.85%	42	149	174
1977	End 1/77	11/02/77	107.46	102.03	90.71	95.10	4.32%	5.16%	31	275	59
1981	02/02/81	09/25/81	135.76	126.91	112.77	122.55	4.82%	14.75%	33	235	97
1982	End 1/82	06/21/82	122.55	120.40	107.20	140.64	6.65%	13.08%	31	141	193
1984	02/03/84	End 11/84	164.93	160.91	163.58	167.24	4.87%	9.73%	34	301	31
1990	End 1/90	End 11/90	353.40	329.08	322.22	330.22	3.39%	7.61%	31	303	31
2000	End 1/00	End 11/00	1469.25	1394.46	1314.95	1320.28	1.05%	5.87%	31	304	31
2001	02/21/01	03/12/01	1320.28	1255.27	1180.16	1148.08	1.14%	4.65%	52	19	294
2002	End 1/02	06/20/02	1148.08	1130.20	1006.29	879.82	1.27%	1.73%	31	140	194
2003	End 1/03	06/11/03	879.82	855.70	997.48	1111.92	2.32%	1.08%	31	131	203
2005	End 1/05	End 11/05	1211.92	1181.27	1249.48	1248.29	1.91%	2.63%	31	303	31

*assumed to be evenly distributed during the year.
#while the WSTL was red.

Exhibit F-2, Panel 2: Calculating the WSTL Returns for Years with Trades

1970

Step 1: Total value of the WSTL's investment in the S&P 500 at the sell signal, end 1/70
S&P 500 closing price + year-to-date dividend earned
$85.02 + (92.06 \times 3.91\%) \times (31 \div 365) =$ — 85.33

Step 2: The buy signal was triggered by the lower limit on 5/14/70.
Add: Interest earned while WSTL was red (measured in terms of the WSTL's
investment in the S&P 500 at the sell signal)
$85.33 \times 6.78\% \times (103 \div 365) =$ — 1.63

Step 3: Total value of the WSTL's investment in 3-month T-bills (measured in terms of
the S&P 500 closing price on the day of the buy signal) — 86.96

Year-end 1970

Step 4: Total value of the WSTL's investment in the S&P 500 at year-end (not including
dividends earned since the buy signal)
Total value from step 3 × Percentage change in S&P 500 since the buy signal
$86.96 \times (92.15 \div 75.44) =$ — 106.22

Step 5: Add: Dividends earned since the buy signal
$86.96 \times 3.91\% \times (231 \div 365) =$ — 2.15

Step 6: Total value of the WSTL's investment in the S&P 500 — 108.37

Step 7: WSTL annual return
Total value from step 6 ÷ S&P 500 closing price at the end of 2000
$(108.37 \div 92.06) - 1.00 =$ — 17.72%

1973

Step 1: Total value of the WSTL's investment in the S&P 500 at the sell signal, 2/01/73
S&P 500 closing price + year-to-date dividend earned
$114.76 + (118.05 \times 2.70\%) \times (32 \div 365) =$ — 115.04

Step 2: The buy signal was triggered by the lower limit on 7/03/73.
Add: Interest earned while WSTL was red (measured in terms of the WSTL's
investment in the S&P 500 at the sell signal)
$115.04 \times 6.08\% \times (152 \div 365) =$ — 2.91

Step 3: Total value of the WSTL's investment in 3-month T-bills (measured in terms of
the S&P 500 closing price on the day of the buy signal) — 117.95

Year-end 1973

Step 4: Total value of the WSTL's investment in the S&P 500 at year-end (not including
dividends earned since the buy signal)
Total value from step 3 × Percentage change in S&P 500 since the buy signal
$117.95 \times (97.55 \div 101.87) =$ — 112.95

Step 5: Add: Dividends earned since the buy signal
$117.95 \times 2.70\% \times (181 \div 365) =$ — 1.58

Step 6: Total value of the WSTL's investment in the S&P 500 — 114.53

Step 7: WSTL annual return
Total value from step 6 ÷ S&P 500 closing price at the end of 2000
$(114.53 \div 118.05) - 1.00 =$ — −2.98%

Exhibit F-2, Panel 2 continues on the next page.

Exhibit F-2: Panel 2 (continued)

1974

Step 1: Total value of the WSTL's investment in the S&P 500 at the sell signal, 2/11/74
S&P 500 closing price + year-to-date dividend earned
90.66 + (97.55 × 3.25%) × (42 ÷ 365) =   91.02

Step 2: The buy signal was triggered by the lower limit on 7/10/74.
Add: Interest earned while WSTL was red (measured in terms of the WSTL's
investment in the S&P 500 at the sell signal)
91.02 × 7.85% × (149 ÷ 365) =   2.92

Step 3: Total value of the WSTL's investment in 3-month T-bills (measured in terms of
the S&P 500 closing price on the day of the buy signal)   93.94

Year-end 1974

Step 4: Total value of the WSTL's investment in the S&P 500 at year-end (not including
dividends earned since the buy signal)
Total value from step 3 × Percentage change in S&P 500 since the buy signal
93.94 × (68.56 ÷ 79.99) =   80.52

Step 5: Add: Dividends earned since the buy signal
93.94 × 3.25% × (174 ÷ 365) =   1.46

Step 6: Total value of the WSTL's investment in the S&P 500   81.98

Step 7: WSTL annual return
Total value from step 6 ÷ S&P 500 closing price at the end of 2000
(81.98 ÷ 97.55) − 1.00 =   −15.96%

1977

Step 1: Total value of the WSTL's investment in the S&P 500 at the sell signal, end 1/77
S&P 500 closing price + year-to-date dividend earned
102.03 + (107.46 × 4.32%) × (31 ÷ 365) =   102.42

Step 2: The buy signal was triggered by the lower limit on 11/02/77.
Add: Interest earned while WSTL was red (measured in terms of the WSTL's
investment in the S&P 500 at the sell signal)
102.42 × 5.16% × (275 ÷ 365) =   3.98

Step 3: Total value of the WSTL's investment in 3-month T-bills (measured in terms of
the S&P 500 closing price on the day of the buy signal)   106.40

Year-end 1977

Step 4: Total value of the WSTL's investment in the S&P 500 at year-end (not including
dividends earned since the buy signal)
Total value from step 3 × Percentage change in S&P 500 since the buy signal
106.40 × (95.10 ÷ 90.71) =   111.55

Step 5: Add: Dividends earned since the buy signal
106.40 × 4.32% × (59 ÷ 365) =   0.74

Step 6: Total value of the WSTL's investment in the S&P 500   112.29

Step 7: WSTL annual return
Total value from step 6 ÷ S&P 500 closing price at the end of 2000
(112.29 ÷ 107.46) − 1.00 =   4.49%

Exhibit F-2: Panel 2 (continued)

1981

Step 1: Total value of the WSTL's investment in the S&P 500 at the sell signal, 2/02/81
S&P 500 closing price + year-to-date dividend earned
126.91 + (135.76 × 4.82%) × (33 ÷ 365) =   127.50

Step 2: The buy signal was triggered by the lower limit on 9/25/81.
Add: Interest earned while WSTL was red (measured in terms of the WSTL's
investment in the S&P 500 at the sell signal)
127.50 × 14.75% × (235 ÷ 365) =   12.11

Step 3: Total value of the WSTL's investment in 3-month T-bills (measured in terms of
the S&P 500 closing price on the day of the buy signal)   139.61

Year-end 1981

Step 4: Total value of the WSTL's investment in the S&P 500 at year-end (not including
dividends earned since the buy signal)
Total value from step 3 × Percentage change in S&P 500 since the buy signal
139.61 × (122.55 ÷ 112.77) =   151.72

Step 5: Add: Dividends earned since the buy signal
139.61 × 4.82% × (97 ÷ 365) =   1.79

Step 6: Total value of the WSTL's investment in the S&P 500   153.51

Step 7: WSTL annual return
Total value from step 6 ÷ S&P 500 closing price at the end of 2000
(153.51 ÷ 135.76) − 1.00 =   13.07%

1982

Step 1: Total value of the WSTL's investment in the S&P 500 at the sell signal, end 1/82
S&P 500 closing price + year-to-date dividend earned
120.40 + (122.55 × 6.65%) × (31 ÷ 365) =   121.09

Step 2: The buy signal was triggered by the lower limit on 6/21/82.
Add: Interest earned while WSTL was red (measured in terms of the WSTL's
investment in the S&P 500 at the sell signal)
121.09 × 13.08% × (141 ÷ 365) =   6.12

Step 3: Total value of the WSTL's investment in 3-month T-bills (measured in terms of
the S&P 500 closing price on the day of the buy signal)   127.21

Year-end 1982

Step 4: Total value of the WSTL's investment in the S&P 500 at year-end (not including
dividends earned since the buy signal)
Total value from step 3 × Percentage change in S&P 500 since the buy signal
127.21 × (140.64 ÷ 107.20) =   166.89

Step 5: Add: Dividends earned since the buy signal
127.21 × 6.65% × (193 ÷ 365) =   4.47

Step 6: Total value of the WSTL's investment in the S&P 500   171.36

Step 7: WSTL annual return
Total value from step 6 ÷ S&P 500 closing price at the end of 2000
(171.36 ÷ 122.55) − 1.00 =   39.83%

Exhibit F-2, Panel 2 continues on the next page.

Exhibit F-2: Panel 2 (continued)

1984

Step 1:	Total value of the WSTL's investment in the S&P 500 at the sell signal, 2/03/84	
	S&P 500 closing price + year-to-date dividend earned	
	160.91 + (164.93 × 4.87%) × (34 ÷ 366) =	161.66
Step 2:	The buy signal was triggered by the time limit at the end 11/84.	
	Add: Interest earned while WSTL was red (measured in terms of the WSTL's	
	investment in the S&P 500 at the sell signal)	
	161.66 × 9.73% × (301 ÷ 366) =	12.94
Step 3:	Total value of the WSTL's investment in 3-month T-bills (measured in terms of	
	the S&P 500 closing price on the day of the buy signal)	174.60

Year-end 1984

Step 4:	Total value of the WSTL's investment in the S&P 500 at year-end (not including	
	dividends earned since the buy signal)	
	Total value from step 3 × Percentage change in S&P 500 since the buy signal	
	174.60 × (167.24 ÷ 163.58) =	178.51
Step 5:	Add: Dividends earned since the buy signal	
	174.60 × 4.87% × (31 ÷ 366) =	0.72
Step 6:	Total value of the WSTL's investment in the S&P 500	179.23
Step 7:	WSTL annual return	
	Total value from step 6 ÷ S&P 500 closing price at the end of 2000	
	(179.23 ÷ 164.93) − 1.00 =	8.67%

1990

Step 1:	Total value of the WSTL's investment in the S&P 500 at the sell signal, end 1/90	
	S&P 500 closing price + year-to-date dividend earned	
	329.08 + (353.40 × 3.39%) × (31 ÷ 365) =	330.10
Step 2:	The buy signal was triggered by the time limit at end 11/90.	
	Add: Interest earned while WSTL was red (measured in terms of the WSTL's	
	investment in the S&P 500 at the sell signal)	
	330.10 × 7.61% × (303 ÷ 365) =	20.85
Step 3:	Total value of the WSTL's investment in 3-month T-bills (measured in terms of	
	the S&P 500 closing price on the day of the buy signal)	350.95

Year-end 1990

Step 4:	Total value of the WSTL's investment in the S&P 500 at year-end (not including	
	dividends earned since the buy signal)	
	Total value from step 3 × Percentage change in S&P 500 since the buy signal	
	350.95 × (330.22 ÷ 322.22) =	359.66
Step 5:	Add: Dividends earned since the buy signal	
	350.95 × 3.39% × (31 ÷ 365) =	1.01
Step 6:	Total value of the WSTL's investment in the S&P 500	360.67
Step 7:	WSTL annual return	
	Total value from step 6 ÷ S&P 500 closing price at the end of 2000	
	(360.67 ÷ 353.40) − 1.00 =	2.06%

Exhibit F-2: Panel 2 (continued)

2000

Step 1:	Total value of the WSTL's investment in the S&P 500 at the sell signal, 1/00 S&P 500 closing price + year-to-date dividend earned $1394.46 + (1469.25 \times 1.05\%) \times (31 \div 366) =$	1395.77
Step 2:	The buy signal was triggered by the time limit at the end 11/00. Add: Interest earned while WSTL was red (measured in terms of the WSTL's investment in the S&P 500 at the sell signal) $1395.77 \times 5.87\% \times (304 \div 366) =$	68.05
Step 3:	Total value of the WSTL's investment in 3-month T-bills (measured in terms of the S&P 500 closing price on the day of the buy signal)	1463.82

Year-end 2000

Step 4:	Total value of the WSTL's investment in the S&P 500 at year-end (not including dividends earned since the buy signal) Total value from step 3 × Percentage change in S&P 500 since the buy signal $1463.82 \times (1320.28 \div 1314.95) =$	1469.75
Step 5:	Add: Dividends earned since the buy signal $1463.82 \times 1.05\% \times (31 \div 366) =$	1.30
Step 6:	Total value of the WSTL's investment in the S&P 500	1471.05
Step 7:	WSTL annual return Total value from step 6 ÷ S&P 500 closing price at the end of 2000 $(1471.05 \div 1469.25) - 1.00 =$	0.12%

2001

Step 1:	Total value of the WSTL's investment in the S&P 500 at the sell signal, 2/21/01 S&P 500 closing price + year-to-date dividend earned $1255.27 + (1320.28 \times 1.14\%) \times (52 \div 365) =$	1257.41
Step 2:	The buy signal was triggered by the lower limit on 3/12/01. Add: Interest earned while WSTL was red (measured in terms of the WSTL's investment in the S&P 500 at the sell signal) $1257.41 \times 4.65\% \times (19 \div 365) =$	3.04
Step 3:	Total value of the WSTL's investment in 3-month T-bills (measured in terms of the S&P 500 closing price on the day of the buy signal)	1260.45

Year-end 2001

Step 4:	Total value of the WSTL's investment in the S&P 500 at year-end (not including dividends earned since the buy signal) Total value from step 3 × Percentage change in S&P 500 since the buy signal $1260.45 \times (1148.08 \div 1180.16) =$	1226.19
Step 5:	Add: Dividends earned since the buy signal $1260.45 \times 1.14\% \times (294 \div 365) =$	11.57
Step 6:	Total value of the WSTL's investment in the S&P 500	1237.76
Step 7:	WSTL annual return Total value from step 6 ÷ S&P 500 closing price at the end of 2000 $(1237.76 \div 1320.28) - 1.00 =$	−6.25%

Exhibit F-2, Panel 2 continues on the next page.

Exhibit F-2: Panel 2 (continued)

2002

Step 1: Total value of the WSTL's investment in the S&P 500 at the sell signal, end 1/02
S&P 500 closing price + year-to-date dividend earned
1130.20 + (1148.08 × 1.27%) × (31 ÷ 365) =   1131.44

Step 2: The buy signal was triggered by the lower limit on 6/20/02.
Add: Interest earned while WSTL was red (measured in terms of the WSTL's
investment in the S&P 500 at the sell signal)
1131.44 × 1.73% × (140 ÷ 365) =   7.51

Step 3: Total value of the WSTL's investment in 3-month T-bills (measured in terms of
the S&P 500 closing price on the day of the buy signal)   1138.95

Year-end 2002

Step 4: Total value of the WSTL's investment in the S&P 500 at year-end (not including
dividends earned since the buy signal)
Total value from step 3 × Percentage change in S&P 500 since the buy signal
1138.95 × (879.82 ÷ 1006.29) =   995.81

Step 5: Add: Dividends earned since the buy signal
1138.95 × 1.27% × (194 ÷ 365) =   7.69

Step 6: Total value of the WSTL's investment in the S&P 500   1003.50

Step 7: WSTL annual return
Total value from step 6 ÷ S&P 500 closing price at the end of 2000
(1003.50 ÷ 1148.08) − 1.00 =   −12.59%

2003

Step 1: Total value of the WSTL's investment in the S&P 500 at the sell signal, end 1/03
S&P 500 closing price + year-to-date dividend earned
855.70 + (879.82 × 2.32%) × (31 ÷ 365) =   857.43

Step 2: The buy signal was triggered by the upper limit on 6/11/03.
Add: Interest earned while WSTL was red (measured in terms of the WSTL's
investment in the S&P 500 at the sell signal)
857.43 × 1.08% × (131 ÷ 365) =   3.32

Step 3: Total value of the WSTL's investment in 3-month T-bills (measured in terms of
the S&P 500 closing price on the day of the buy signal)   860.75

Year-end 2003

Step 4: Total value of the WSTL's investment in the S&P 500 at year-end (not including
dividends earned since the buy signal)
Total value from step 3 × Percentage change in S&P 500 since the buy signal
860.75 × (1111.92 ÷ 997.48) =   959.50

Step 5: Add: Dividends earned since the buy signal
860.75 × 2.32% × (203 ÷ 365) =   11.11

Step 6: Total value of the WSTL's investment in the S&P 500   970.61

Step 7: WSTL annual return
Total value from step 6 ÷ S&P 500 closing price at the end of 2000
(970.61 ÷ 879.82) − 1.00 =   10.32%

Exhibit F-2: Panel 2 (continued)

2005

Step 1: Total value of the WSTL's investment in the S&P 500 at the sell signal, end 1/05
S&P 500 closing price + year-to-date dividend earned
$$1181.27 + (1211.92 \times 1.91\%) \times (31 \div 365) = \qquad 1183.24$$

Step 2: The buy signal was triggered by the time limit at end 11/05.
Add: Interest earned while WSTL was red (measured in terms of the WSTL's
investment in the S&P 500 at the sell signal)
$$1183.24 \times 2.63\% \times (303 \div 365) = \qquad 25.83$$

Step 3: Total value of the WSTL's investment in 3-month T-bills (measured in terms of
the S&P 500 closing price on the day of the buy signal) \qquad 1209.07

Year-end 2005

Step 4: Total value of the WSTL's investment in the S&P 500 at year-end (not including
dividends earned since the buy signal)
Total value from step 3 × Percentage change in S&P 500 since the buy signal
$$1209.07 \times (1248.29 \div 1249.48) = \qquad 1207.92$$

Step 5: Add: Dividends earned since the buy signal
$$1209.07 \times 1.91\% \times (31 \div 365) = \qquad 1.96$$

Step 6: Total value of the WSTL's investment in the S&P 500 \qquad 1209.88

Step 7: WSTL annual return
Total value from step 6 ÷ S&P 500 closing price at the end of 2000
$$(1209.88 \div 1211.92) - 1.00 = \qquad -0.17\%$$

Appendix G

◇◇◇◇◇◇◇◇◇◇◇◇◇◇◇

ANNUAL RETURNS FOR THE WSTL AND S&P 500, CLASSIFIED BY TIER, 1935-2006

Exhibit G-1

Annual Returns for the WSTL and S&P 500, Classified by Tier, 1935-2006

The years within each tier are listed chronologically.

Row	Two-Year Period	S&P 500 Two-Year Mean Annual Return	Year	Type of Year	WSTL Return	S&P 500 Return	Outcome of Trade
				Year Immediately after Two-Year Period			
		Tier 1: Two-Year Mean Annual Return Above 13.6%					
1	1933-34	26.3%	1935	1C	65.4%	47.7%	17.7%
2	1934-35	23.1%	1936	1A	33.9%	33.9%	
3	1935-36	40.8%	1937	1B	−32.0%	−35.0%	3.0%
4	1938-39	15.4%	1940	1C	3.1%	−9.8%	12.9%
5	1942-43	23.1%	1944	1A	19.8%	19.8%	
6	1943-44	22.8%	1945	1A	36.4%	36.4%	
7	1944-45	28.1%	1946	1B	1.3%	−8.1%	9.4%
8	1945-46	14.2%	1947	1B	8.3%	5.7%	2.6%
9	1949-50	25.3%	1951	1A	24.0%	24.0%	
10	1950-51	27.9%	1952	1A	18.4%	18.4%	
11	1951-52	21.2%	1953	1C	8.5%	−1.0%	9.5%
12	1953-54	25.8%	1955	1A	31.6%	31.6%	
13	1954-55	42.1%	1956	1C	2.6%	6.6%	−4.0%
14	1955-56	19.1%	1957	1C	1.2%	−10.8%	11.9%*
15	1957-58	16.3%	1959	1A	12.0%	12.0%	
16	1958-59	27.7%	1960	1C	0.0%	0.5%	−0.5%
17	1960-61	13.7%	1962	1C	2.3%	−8.7%	11.0%*
18	1963-64	19.6%	1965	1A	12.5%	12.5%	
19	1964-65	14.5%	1966	1B	−1.3%	−10.1%	8.8%
20	1967-68	17.5%	1969	1C	5.8%	−8.5%	14.3%
21	1971-72	16.6%	1973	1C	−3.0%	−14.7%	11.7%

*This difference does not add across due to rounding

Exhibit G-1 continues on the next page.

151

Exhibit G-1: Tier 1 (continued)

Row	Two-Year Period	S&P 500 Two-Year Mean Annual Return	Year	Type of Year	WSTL Return	S&P 500 Return	Outcome of Trade
				Year Immediately after Two-Year Period			
22	1975-76	30.5%	1977	1C	4.5%	−7.2%	11.7%
23	1979-80	25.4%	1981	1C	13.1%	−4.9%	18.0%
24	1980-81	13.8%	1982	1C	39.8%	21.4%	18.4%
25	1982-83	22.0%	1984	1C	8.7%	6.3%	2.4%
26	1983-84	14.4%	1985	1A	32.2%	32.2%	
27	1984-85	19.2%	1986	1A	18.5%	18.5%	
28	1985-86	25.3%	1987	1A	5.2%	5.2%	
29	1988-89	24.2%	1990	1C	2.1%	−3.2%	5.2%*
30	1989-90	14.2%	1991	1A	30.6%	30.6%	
31	1990-91	13.7%	1992	1A	7.7%	7.7%	
32	1991-92	19.1%	1993	1A	10.0%	10.0%	
33	1994-95	19.4%	1996	1A	23.1%	23.1%	
34	1995-96	30.3%	1997	1A	33.4%	33.4%	
35	1996-97	28.2%	1998	1A	28.6%	28.6%	
36	1997-98	31.0%	1999	1A	21.0%	21.0%	
37	1998-99	24.8%	2000	1C	0.1%	−9.1%	9.2%
38	2003-04	19.8%	2005	1C	−0.2%	4.9%	−5.1%
Mean for Tier 1 years					**13.9%**	**9.5%**	**8.4%**

*This difference does not add across due to rounding.

Tier 2: Two-Year Mean Annual Return From 6.2% to 13.6%

Row	Two-Year Period	S&P 500 Two-Year Mean Annual Return	Year	Type of Year	WSTL Return	S&P 500 Return	Outcome of Trade
39	1948-49	12.1%	1950	Tier 2	31.7%	31.7%	
40	1952-53	8.7%	1954	Tier 2	52.6%	52.6%	
41	1959-60	6.2%	1961	Tier 2	26.9%	26.9%	
42	1961-62	9.1%	1963	Tier 2	22.8%	22.8%	
43	1962-63	7.0%	1964	Tier 2	16.5%	16.5%	
44	1966-67	7.0%	1968	Tier 2	11.1%	11.1%	
45	1970-71	9.2%	1972	Tier 2	19.0%	19.0%	
46	1976-77	8.3%	1978	Tier 2	6.6%	6.6%	
47	1978-79	12.5%	1980	Tier 2	32.4%	32.4%	
48	1981-82	8.3%	1983	Tier 2	22.5%	22.5%	
49	1986-87	11.9%	1988	Tier 2	16.8%	16.8%	
50	1987-88	11.0%	1989	Tier 2	31.5%	31.5%	
51	1992-93	8.8%	1994	Tier 2	1.3%	1.3%	
52	2004-05	7.9%	2006	Tier 2	15.8%	15.8%	
Mean for Tier 2 years					**22.0%**	**22.0%**	

Exhibit G-1 (continued)

Row	Two-Year Period	S&P 500 Two-Year Mean Annual Return	Year Immediately after Two-Year Period				
			Year	Type of Year	WSTL Return	S&P 500 Return	Outcome of Trade
	**Tier 3: Two-Year Mean Annual Return Below 6.2%**
53	1936-37	−0.6%	1938	3B	42.7%	31.1%	11.5%*
54	1937-38	−2.0%	1939	3C	13.1%	−0.4%	13.5%
55	1939-40	−5.1%	1941	3C	−8.0%	−11.6%	3.6%
56	1940-41	−10.7%	1942	3B	26.2%	20.3%	5.9%
57	1941-42	4.4%	1943	3A	25.9%	25.9%	
58	1946-47	−1.2%	1948	3C	0.9%	5.5%	−4.7%*
59	1947-48	5.6%	1949	3B	27.0%	18.8%	8.3%*
60	1956-57	−2.1%	1958	3A	43.4%	43.4%	
61	1965-66	1.2%	1967	3A	24.0%	24.0%	
62	1968-69	1.3%	1970	3C	17.7%	4.0%	13.7%
63	1969-70	−2.2%	1971	3A	14.3%	14.3%	
64	1972-73	2.2%	1974	3C	−16.0%	−26.5%	10.5%
65	1973-74	−20.6%	1975	3A	37.2%	37.2%	
66	1974-75	5.4%	1976	3A	23.8%	23.8%	
67	1977-78	−0.3%	1979	3A	18.4%	18.4%	
68	1993-94	5.6%	1995	3A	37.4%	37.4%	
69	1999-00	6.0%	2001	3B	−6.3%	−11.9%	5.6%
70	2000-01	−10.5%	2002	3C	−12.6%	−22.1%	9.5%
71	2001-02	−17.0%	2003	3C	10.3%	28.7%	−18.4%
72	2002-03	3.3%	2004	3A	10.9%	10.9%	
Mean for Tier 3 years					16.5%	13.6%	5.4%

*This difference does not add across due to rounding.

ENDNOTES

1. In this book, "important terms to know" appear in boldface type where they are defined. **S&P 500** is the first of those terms. All of the important terms to know comprise the Glossary at the end of the book.

2. The S&P 500 has consisted of 500 stocks since March 5, 1957; before that it consisted of 90 stocks. For convenience, "S&P 500" will be used in this book for the entire 1935-2006 period.

3. Kenneth L. Fisher, *The Only Three Questions That Count: Investing by Knowing What Others Don't* (Wiley, 2007), p. 277.

4. John C. Bogle, *Common Sense on Mutual Funds* (Wiley, 1999), p. 20.

5. Peter Lynch, *One Up on Wall Street* (Simon & Schuster, 1989), p. 74.

6. Hartman L. Butler, Jr., "An Hour with Mr. Graham," in Janet Lowe, *The Rediscovered Benjamin Graham* (Wiley, 1999), p. 273.

7. Scott Patterson, *The Wall Street Journal* (January 23, 2007), p. C1.

8. John C. Bogle, *Common Sense on Mutual Funds* (Wiley, 1999), p. 6.

9. An appendix to Chapter 9 sets forth the specifications for buy signals.

10. I thank Peter Eliades, editor of the *Stockmarket Cycles* newsletter, for bringing the ulcer index to my attention.

11. Daniel Kahneman and Amos Tversky, "Prospect Theory: An Analysis of Decision Under Risk." *Econometrica* (March 1979), pp. 263-292; and Richard H. Thaler, Amos Tversky, Daniel Kahneman and Alan Schwarts, The Effect of Myopia and Loss Aversion on Risk Taking: An Experimental Test," *Quarterly Journal of Economics* (May 1997), pp. 647-661.

12. William F. Sharpe, Gordon J. Alexander, and Jeffery V. Bailey, *Investments*, 6th edition (Prentice Hall, 1999), p. 96.

13. Mark H. Williamson, Invesco newsletter (Summer 2001), p. 2.

14. Both Fidelity and Vanguard offer even lower-cost shares to index-fund investors who have a fund balance of at least $100,000.

15. More than three million people at education, research and some other nonprofit institutions have a retirement account at TIAA-CREF, one of the world's largest retirement systems. While TIAA-CREF does not offer an S&P 500 index fund, it offers the CREF Equity Index Fund. This fund tracks the Russell 3000, which accounts for approximately 98% of the total value of the U.S. stock market. (The S&P 500 accounts for some 75% of the total value of the U.S. stock market.) For the 10-year period through 2006, the average annual return for the Russell 3000 was 10.06% compared to the S&P 500's 10.02%. On average for that period, the CREF Equity Index Fund trailed the Russell 3000 by 0.28% per year. That means the total cost of owning the CREF Equity Index fund was less than 8¢ a day per $10,000 of market value in the investor's account.

16. Be aware that, in addition to the brokerage commission, the buyer and seller in an S&P 500 ETF transaction each incur the cost of the "bid-ask spread" (the difference between the ETF's purchase price and its slightly lower selling price), which is the profit earned by the market-maker firm that handles the order. The cost of the bid-ask spread tends to be less than 0.05% of the total amount of the transaction.

17. John C. Bogle, *Bogle on Mutual Funds* (Irwin, 1994), p. 61.

18. Dennis K. Berman, *The Wall Street Journal* (September 11, 2007), p. C3.

19. For example, see Eugene F. Fama, "The Behavior of Stock Market Prices," *Journal of Business* (January 1965), pp. 34-105.

20. Larry E. Swedroe, *What Wall Street Doesn't Want You To Know* (St. Martin's Press, 2001), p. 36.

21. Using regression analysis, the correlation between the S&P 500's price change in a given year and the previous year in Exhibit 11-1 is virtually nil; r^2 between the two variables is a mere 0.1%.

22. Eugene F. Fama, "The Behavior of Stock Market Prices," *Journal of Business* (January 1965), p 35.

23. Eugene F. Fama, "Efficient Capital Markets: A Review of Theory and Empirical Work," *Journal of Finance* (May 1970), p. 388.

24. Dalbar initially reported that stock fund investors earned an average annual return of only 2.6% for 1984-2002, but the return was recalculated after a bias in the study's methodology was found. See Jonathan Clements, *The Wall Street Journal* (March 31, 2004), p. D1.

25. Burton G. Malkiel, *A Random Walk Down Wall Street* (Norton, 1990), p. 179.

26. William A. Sherden, *The Fortune Sellers* (Wiley, 1998), p. 105.

27. John R. Dorfman, *The Wall Street Journal* (January 30, 1997), p. C1.

28. Robin Goldwyn Blumenthal, *Barron's* (July 17, 2000), p. 28.

29. Bear Markets: A Historical Perspective on Market Downturns (an educational booklet), The Vanguard Group (March 1997), p. 8.

30. John C. Bogle, *Common Sense on Mutual Finds* (Wiley, 1999), p. 20.

31. Burton G. Malkiel, *A Random Walk Down Wall Stree*t (Norton, 2003), p. 27.

32. William J. Bernstein, *The Four Pillars of Investing* (McGraw Hill, 2002), p. 231.

33. "Peter Lynch on Investing," Fidelity Investments website (November 24, 2002).

34. Hartman L. Butler, Jr., "An Hour with Mr. Graham," in Janet Lowe, *The Rediscovered Benjamin Graham* (Wiley, 1999), p. 273.

35. T. Rowe Price newsletter (Fall 1987), p. 1.

36. Austin Pryor, *A Special Report Prepared for the Sound Mind Investing Family of Readers*, (1999), p. 7.

37. Burton G. Malkiel, *The Wall Street Journal* (April 4, 2000), p. A24.

38. Burton G. Malkiel, *A Random Walk Down Wall Street*, (Norton, 2003), p. 165.

39. Peter Lynch managed Fidelity's Magellan Fund from 1977 to 1990. Amazingly during that time, he earned approximately *3.7 times more total return than the S&P 500.* Lynch invested primarily in stocks of smaller, lesser known companies. On a risk-adjusted basis (that is, reducing his returns to compensate for the higher risk of smaller stocks), Lynch's performance was far and away the best of any mutual fund manager in history. Proponents of the efficient market theory explain Lynch's market-beating performance by saying either (1) he used his exceptional ability to exploit a rather inefficient market in which many of the companies in his portfolio had not attracted much attention from investment analysts or (2) he was simply lucky for 14 years, a period that is too short to qualify as the long-term.

40. John J. Murphy, *Technical Analysis of the Financial Markets* (New York Institute of Finance, 1999), p. 27.

41. The WSTL strategy has one sell signal and one buy signal—that is, one round-trip trade—in each 1B, 1C, 3B and 3C year. Based on the S&P 500's movements during 1935-1969, any set of rules for having more than one round-trip trade in those years would have diminished the WSTL returns.

GLOSSARY

◇◇◇◇◇◇◇◇◇◇◇◇◇◇◇◇◇

The Glossary is limited to the important terms to know that are in boldface type in this book.

Alpha. The difference between the performance of a professional money manager (or a market-timing model such as the WSTL) and the performance of an appropriate benchmark (such as the S&P 500). (p. 10)

Asset allocation. Deciding on and maintaining a suitable mix of different types of investments in your portfolio. (p. 54)

Back-tested (Back-testing). Applying a market-timing model to the same period from which it was developed. (p. 41)

Benchmark. An appropriate standard (such as the S&P 500) against which the performance of an investment strategy can be judged. (p. 10)

CAGR. See *compound annual growth rate.*

Category. A core concept of the WSTL model used in classifying years; specifically, it is a set of conditions for the S&P 500's movement during part or all of the January-through-April period, in relation to its December low of the prior year. (p. 14)

Category "A" year. This classification occurs when the S&P 500 meets either of two conditions: (1) the lowest daily closing price during the prior year's December (the December low) is not broken during the January-through-April period of the year in question, meaning that none of the S&P 500's daily closing prices during the January-through-April period were lower than the December low, or (2) the prior year's December low is broken during January (but was not broken during the February-through-April period) of the year being classified and January's price change is positive. The classification is established at the end of April. (p. 16)

Category "B" year. This classification occurs when the S&P 500 meets two conditions: (1) the prior year's December low is broken during the February-through-April period of the year being classified, and (2) January's price change is positive. (It doesn't matter whether the December low is broken during January.) The classification is established on a particular day during the February-through-April period. (p. 16)

Category "C" year. This classification occurs when the S&P 500 meets two conditions: (1) the prior year's December low is broken during the January-through-April period of the year being classified, and (2) January's price change is negative. The classification is established on a particular day between the end of January and the end of April. (p. 17)

Compound annual growth rate (CAGR). The average annual rate of return that, when compounded over time, accounts for the change in the total value of an investment from the beginning of a period to the end of the period, assuming that there were no withdrawals and no additional investments. Mathematically, the CAGR is the geometric mean. (p. 29)

Dollar-cost averaging. Investing a set amount of money at regular intervals, such as making monthly contributions to your 401(k). (p. 54)

Dow trifecta. This phenomenon occurs when three Dow Jones averages—the Industrials, the Transports and the Utilities—all hit an all-time high on the same day. (p. 24)

Efficient financial market. In this type of market, the prices incorporate all available information, which means that prices change only in response to new information. (p. 92)

Efficient market theory. This theory holds that prices in financial markets move in a random and unpredictable path through time, because each item of new information will be random in regard to being better or worse than market participants had expected. Consequently, past movements of stock prices (for either an individual stock or a group of stocks such as the S&P 500) are a completely unreliable basis for forecasting future stock prices in any way that would make risk-adjusted returns greater than the returns under the buy-and-hold strategy. (p. 92)

ETF. See *exchange-traded fund.*

Exchange policy. The rules established by a mutual fund company that govern the transactions (purchases and sales) involving its individual mutual funds. Examples include: (1) a redemption fee of 0.50% paid by the seller if the fund has been held for less than 90 days and (2) a restriction against repurchase of a fund within 60 days after selling it. (p. 51)

Exchange-traded fund (ETF). A passively managed fund that mimics the performance of a particular index, such as the S&P 500. This type of fund trades on an exchange throughout the day like a stock. (p. 51)

Favorable part of the presidential cycle. The October-through-December period of years 1 and 2 of the cycle plus all of years 3 and 4, or a total of 30 months (62.5%) of the 48-month cycle. (p. 40)

Index mutual fund. A passively managed fund that mimics the performance of a particular index, such as the S&P 500. This type of fund is priced once a day when the U.S. financial markets close at 4 p.m. eastern time. (p. 51)

Market anomaly. Any investment strategy that has generated abnormal returns—returns which, after being adjusted for risk, exceeded the market's mean return over a long period. (p. 39)

1A year. A type of year in the WSTL model; the year is both in Tier 1 and category A. (p. 15)

1B year. A type of year in the WSTL model; the year is both in Tier 1 and category B. (p. 15)

1C year. A type of year in the WSTL model; the year is both in Tier 1 and category C. (p. 15)

Out-of-sample period. See *test period.*

Profitable trade. For the period when the WSTL is red, the S&P 500 return is less than the interest the WSTL investor earns on 3-month Treasury bills or in a money market fund. That means for the year in which a profitable trade occurs, the WSTL return is greater than the S&P 500 return. (p. 8)

Return. The change in an investment's value (including reinvested dividends) for a specified period, stated as a percent of its value at the beginning of the period. (p. 6)

Reversion to the mean. A strong force in the stock market (and all other financial markets) under which periods of high returns have a tendency to occur after periods of lower returns, and periods of high returns tend to be followed by periods of lower returns. The result is that returns over, say, any 20-year period tend to have an arithmetic average return (a mean) which is nearly the same as their long-term mean. (p. 4)

Risk. The uncertainty regarding the future value of an investment. In the practical application of this definition, investors mainly concern themselves with the possibility of an investment losing money. (p. 7)

Sample period. 1935-1969, the period from which the S&P 500's annual returns and short-term movements were used to develop the WSTL model. (p. 5)

S&P 500. The broad-based, large-company index that comprises approximately 75% of the total value of the U.S. stock market. The S&P 500 is broad based because it includes stocks from all of the major sectors of the U.S. economy. The S&P 500 has consisted of 500 stocks since March 5, 1957; before then it consisted of 90 stocks. For convenience, "S&P 500" is used in this book for the entire 1935-2006 period. (p. 3)

S&P 500 price change. The percentage change in the S&P 500's price for a given period; for example, the S&P 500 closed at 1248.29 at the end of 2005 and closed at 1418.30 at the end of 2006, so its price change for 2006 was 13.6% [(1418.30 − 1248.29) ÷ 1248.29 = 13.6%]. (p. 7)

S&P 500 reinvested dividends. The compounded value of the dividends paid by companies comprising the S&P 500, expressed as a percentage for a given year. (p. 7)

S&P 500 return. The S&P 500's price change plus its reinvested dividends; as an example, for 2006 the S&P 500's price change was 13.6% and its reinvested dividends were 2.2%, so the return was 15.8%. (p. 7)

Spiders. The pronunciation for SPDRs, which stands for Standard & Poor's Depository Receipts. This is the largest exchange-traded fund that mimics the S&P 500. (p. 51)

Standard deviation. A statistical measure of the extent to which the returns of an investment strategy fluctuate over time. The less an investment strategy's returns vary from year to year in relation to its mean annual return for the period studied, the smaller the standard deviation and the lower the risk. (p. 32)

Taking the heat. Whenever the WSTL investor has missed out on the S&P 500's net gain at any point during a period in which the WSTL is red. Taking the heat increases in direct proportion to the size of the S&P 500's net gain. (p. 58)

Test period. 1970-2006, the period used to evaluate the WSTL's performance (that is, its returns and risk). Also called *out-of-sample period*. (p. 5)

thewallstreettrafficlight.com. The companion website for this book. The website has three purposes: (1) to save you the time that would be required to determine the buy and sell signals yourself, (2) to keep you updated on the performance of the WSTL strategy compared to the strategy of buying-and-holding the S&P 500 starting with 2007 and (3) to provide you educational material that complements the contents of this book. (p. 50)

3A year. A type of year in the WSTL model; the year is both in Tier 3 and category A. (p. 15)

3B year. A type of year in the WSTL model; the year is both in Tier 3 and category B. (p. 15)

3C year. A type of year in the WSTL model; the year is both in Tier 3 and category C. (p. 15)

Tier. A core concept of the WSTL model used in classifying years; specifically, it is a range of the S&P 500's average (mean) return for the two-year period immediately preceding the year being classified. (p. 14)

Tier 1 year. The S&P 500's average (mean) return for the two-year period immediately preceding the year being classified is above 13.6%. (p. 14)

Tier 2 year. The S&P 500's average (mean) return for the two-year period immediately preceding the year being classified is in the 6.2% to 13.6% range. The category A, B or C classification is not applicable to a Tier 2 year. (p. 14)

Tier 3 year. The S&P 500's average (mean) return for the two-year period immediately preceding the year being classified is below 6.2%. (p. 14)

Type of year. A core concept of the WSTL model; there are seven types of years—1A, 1B, 1C, Tier 2, 3A, 3B and 3C. (p. 15)

Ulcer index. A comprehensive measure of an investment strategy's risk. It takes into account the "ulcer causing potential" of the depth and duration of declines in a strategy's market value from its beginning value until each subsequent new high (if any) occurred through the period studied. The less the depth of declines in a strategy's market value and the shorter they are, the smaller the ulcer index and the lower risk. (p. 32)

Unfavorable part of the presidential cycle. The January-through-September period of years 1 and 2 of the cycle, or a total of 18 months (37.5%) of the 48-month cycle. (p. 40)

Unprofitable trade. For the period when the WSTL is red, the S&P 500 return is greater than the interest the WSTL investor earns on 3-month Treasury bills or in a money market fund. That means for the year in which an unprofitable trade occurs, the WSTL return is less than the S&P 500 return. (p. 8)